1909–2009

FROM COASTAL SAIL TO GLOBAL SHIPPING

The History of The Steamship Mutual Underwriting Association Limited

Helen Doe

Published by Steamship Insurance Management Services Ltd

The right of Helen Doe to be identified as the author of this work has been asserted in accordance with sections 77 and 78 of the Copyright, Designs and Patents Act 1988

First published 2009

Steamship Insurance Management Services Ltd

ISBN 978-0-9563097-0-9

Design www.designbystructure.com

Printed and bound by Toppan, China

ISBN 978-0-9563097-0-9

9 780956 309709

CONTENTS

List of Illustrations

Foreword

Steamship has been extremely fortunate to persuade Dr Helen Doe, an academic historian specialising in the maritime field, to write this brief history of the Club's first 100 years. As an enduring part of a wider programme of celebrations in our major markets, the Directors and Managers wanted to publish a book which both celebrated the Club's achievements over the last century and also documented Steamship's progress from a small regional club to a diverse global organisation accurately and objectively, placing it in the context of the wider historical landscape. I hope you will agree that the author has fulfilled that brief admirably.

Given that the bulk of the material at her disposal was the rather dry and dusty minute books of Committee and Board meetings and such ledgers as have survived four office moves and two world wars, Dr Doe has managed to craft an attractive and eminently accessible account of how the Club reached its current position. Fortunately, her task was made at least a little easier by the generosity, both in terms of time and material, of the numerous contributors from Steamship's past who have responded with personal reminiscences or the memorabilia and written recollections of those members of their family who were involved in the Club's story over the years. I would like to add my personal thanks to those of Dr Doe for their help and generosity.

From my perspective, as someone who has spent a little over half their life working for Steamship and been involved in almost a third of its history, one of the most fascinating aspects that this account has revealed is just how much of Steamship's current approach and priorities derive directly from the Club's early development and the pre-occupations of its early Managers, particularly Sydney Crowe. 'Service' and 'diversity' have been persistent themes running through at least the last 60 or 70 years of the Club's journey to becoming a truly international P&I Club. The other recurrent thread is the way in which being one of the more recent entrants into the world of P&I has encouraged Steamship to be both pioneering and innovative in its search for growth and success.

Perhaps less parochially, I think Dr Doe has used Steamship's story very skillfully to provide fascinating insights into some of the main elements which have motivated and driven change both in the interwoven progress of shipping and P&I and the interdependent relationship of Club and shipowner over the last century. I hope others will enjoy this highly readable account as much as I have.

James Stockdale, Senior Partner

Acknowledgements

Completing this book in the timescale has been enjoyable and challenging. One hundred years of minutes to be examined and people, additional archive material and illustrations to be traced. An early decision was to examine the key steps in Steamship's transformation from a tiny insurance club to an international player and so some technical aspects of the world of mutual marine insurance have been omitted, together with events that have affected all Clubs. It is also inevitably an internal view of one organisation rather than an analysis of mutual clubs in general.

That the book has been completed within the timescale is due in no small measure to the assistance of many people. The staff of the following libraries and archives have been very helpful; Bartlett Library of the National Maritime Museum Cornwall, Lloyd's Register, Guildhall Library, Priaulx Library in Guernsey, the Centre for Kentish Studies in Maidstone and, the Whitstable Library. David Raddings, Jason Whitaker, John Seagrove, David Asprey, Jonathan Varcoe, Dr Roy Fenton, Dr Stig Tenold, Dr Mathias Reiss, Peter Thomson and others gave assistance in various ways.

Of the many people in or connected with Steamship my thanks go to them for their help. Chris Adams, Jonathan Andrews, and Anthony Warren all gave much assistance. Lanfranco Spechel sent a charming memoir of his time in London. Tony Jones in SSM Bermuda had a chance encounter with Richard Plincke, son of John Plincke. Margaret Webb (formerly Tolhurst) provided information and introduced me to Bridget Wayman (née Howard-Smith). While Anthony and Peter Crowe provided pictures and information on their father as did Julian Morgan, Sandy Struthers and Chris Ahrenkiel about their fathers. Herman Boettjer of Sloman Neptun provided some excellent documents and pictures as did Mr Dhanki of Crowe Boda. George Greenwood, Doreen McDonnell, Peter Hicks, Larry Cork and Dave Gurton all met with me. Mention must go to David Hooper whose painstaking transcription of the early minutes up to 1950 saved a great deal of time and to Richard Stace who was an enthusiastic supporter. John Mace of the International Group patiently answered queries and located articles. Several of the current Directors of Steamship including Mr Otto Fritzner, the Chairman of Steamship Mutual Bermuda, kindly answered my questions.

I am particularly grateful to James Stockdale and Gary Rynsard who have been more than helpful in providing me with access to material and allowed me to write my own view of their history. Finally, Jackie Callard has been an essential figure and she worked very hard to smooth my path, track down people and ensure that the book was published on time.

Helen Doe

Chapter 1

THE SAILING SHIP FAMILY OF CLUBS

The origins of the Club and the men who established it.
Its development from a small west country base to a national London
based club insuring the last of the coastal sailing ships.

The Steamship Mutual Underwriting Association Limited was established on 16th October 1909. The legal documents to set up the Club under English law were drawn up by a firm of lawyers in the City of London, W & W Stocken of 3 & 4 Lime Street Square. Seven men signed the articles of association setting up the Club and they were an interesting mixture of backgrounds and ages. Arthur Reiner, aged 25, was a merchant based at 40 Bishopsgate Street. Of Romanian birth he had just two years earlier become a naturalised British citizen.[1] R A Ramsay gave his occupation as a gentleman and his address as an office premises in the city. Ramsay was part of Ramsay Brothers who were stock jobbers based in the city. Herbert Pope of Kingston-upon-Thames was a surveyor. Then there was Augustus Hobbs, aged 65 and a solicitor. He gave his status as gentleman and his address as a flat in Highbury. Charles Henry Nurse, aged 47, and Alexander Johns, aged 53, were both Gloucester shipowners. Finally Lionel Clark Sage, aged 28, is named as the Secretary to the new association and he gave his address as Kingston Hill, Surrey.

There is one more name who was to become very important to the development of the Club, but who was just at this stage a witness to the signatures of Hobbs, Johns and Nurse, and that was Alfred Stocken, aged 29. Alfred gave his address as Teddington and his occupation as gentleman. He was, in fact, a lawyer in his father, Walter's, firm of W & W Stocken. So here were the eight men who came together to establish a new mutual marine insurance club for steamships, but why did they set up the new association and what brought them together?

Sage, Stocken, Johns and Nurse were not strangers to one another as they were already business associates in the Sailing Ship Mutual Association which had been established in 1906. Indeed Charles Nurse was the chairman, Johns was on the committee and Sage was the manager with Stocken as the legal advisor. In the agreement for Steamship the wording gives Lionel Sage the credit for setting up the new Club. 'Whereas the said Managers (L C Sage) have been instrumental in establishing the said association and been requested to act as Managers.'[2] It was at his premises in Lime Street Square where the new Club was based. The entry for Sage in the London Trade directory was as 'London Sailing Ship Mutual Protection Association (L C Sage & Co Managers)' and, just in case the nature of the business was in doubt from its name, it was further described as providing 'Mutual Protection of sailing vessels'.[3]

Mutual marine insurance is where shipowners come together to insure each others' ships and share risks and it has been in existence for centuries. Originally it was confined to regular trades, such as coal and timber, and developed from 'the confidence which shipowners entertained in each other'.[4] The groups were small, everyone knew each other and an annual premium was paid and that became the fund out of which claims were settled with further calls on members should the need arise. Administration costs were kept low, often with just a part-time secretariat, and the Clubs operated on a non-profit basis. By the early nineteenth century there were many such Clubs based around the British coast.[5]

Initially these only insured the hull of the ship, but during the nineteenth century public attitudes about risk began to change as a result of high-profile railway accidents. This led to calls for individuals or their relatives to be able to sue for damages and liabilities increased, particularly at a time of increased numbers of emigrant ships. Additionally with greater numbers of ships, and the change to iron and steam and larger vessels, port

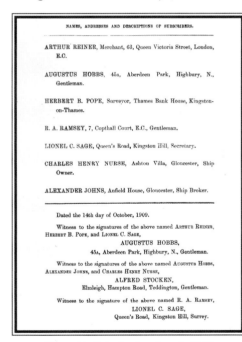

Steamship Mutual subscribers in 1909

Crystal Spring schooner ashore

[1] The National Archives: PRO HO 144/849/149765 naturalisation papers Arthur Reiner; *Kelly's Post Office Directory London* 1909

[2] Steamship Mutual Memorandum and Articles, Schedule A

[3] *Kelly's Post Office Directory London* 1909

[4] British Parliamentary Papers; Select Committee on Marine Insurance, 1810

[5] Sarah Palmer, 'The Indemnity in the London Marine Insurance Market, 1824-50' in Oliver M Westall (ed) *The Historian and the Business of Insurance* (Manchester: Manchester University Press, 1984), 74-94 (pp 78-79)

Helena Tregenza, 155-ton schooner owned by C&F Nurse

authorities became increasingly concerned about damage to infrastructure and wreck removal. In 1855 the first Protection and Indemnity (P&I) Clubs were formed and these, again, were mutual clubs.[6]

Of the signatories to the new mutual insurance Club, only Charles Nurse and Alexander Johns were shipowners. Johns owned the *Excelsior, John Sims, Laura Quin, Lizzie* and *Queen of Clippers*. Nurse solely owned two ships, *Helena Tregenza* and *Mary & Elizabeth* but also had an interest in *John Gibson, Sunshine, Vim, Victor, Waft, Welsh Belle* and *C & F Nurse*. It might be expected that all of these were steamships, since that was the stated aim of the new Club, however every single one was a sailing vessel and they were all insured with the Sailing Ship Mutual Association.[7] So, not one member of the group of men who established The Steamship Mutual Underwriting Association Limited was a steamship owner. It seems that the Club was set up to address a potential business opportunity for the men involved as most of them, including Nurse who was also a shipbroker, could gain from commissions related to the new Club.

The articles of the new Club allowed Committee members three guineas (a guinea was £1 1s) for attendance and those not living near London could claim two guineas per day for being occupied in travelling plus reasonable travelling expenses. Brokers were paid 5 per cent of premiums for introductions, while the Managers received five shillings in the pound for insurance of any member in Classes 1, 2, 3 (all risks, total loss and total loss and general average) and 6 (freight), and entrance fees for members entered in Classes 4 (Protection, Indemnity, Workmen's Compensation Act, Freight Demurrage and Defence) and 5 (Three-fourths Damage done).[8] The definition of a ship included 'boats, barges and floating vessels of every description whether British or foreign', but did not, except in the Club's title, specifically mention steamships.

If it was an act of business opportunism then the new Club was entering a busy market. For steamships there were of course the large well established clubs such as Shipowners,

British Marine Mutual, Britannia and the UK Club. Perhaps the establishment of the new Steamship Mutual Club by the Chairman, a Committee member and the manager of the Sailing Ship Mutual Association, was recognition of the realities of shipping. Even the most dedicated sailing shipowner could see where the future lay, and Steamship was designed to be a new competitor. However it would make more sense if the men involved were well involved with steamships since this is the way in which most mutual clubs were set up, by the very owners who needed to provide mutual insurance. Trust, knowledge of the business, mutual support for one another and being prepared to share mutual risks were essential.

Mutual Insurance and the Sailing Ship Mutual Family

The new Club was a very junior partner to the Sailing Ship Mutual Insurance Association through which it was re-insured. Sailing Ship Mutual was incorporated on 14th February 1906 and, as its name suggests, was founded to look after the interests of the remaining small sailing ships that were still active despite the dominance of steam. Almost all business was done in the name of Sailing Ship and the references to Steamship are few until the 1920s. The business affairs and the committees of both clubs were so intertwined it is hard to separate them. Claims that should have been discussed in Steamship were discussed in Sailing Ship and no lists of ships entered between 1909 and 1950 survive for either Club. These early years are therefore the story of the Sailing Ship Mutual family, which would, by 1919, consist of four Clubs.

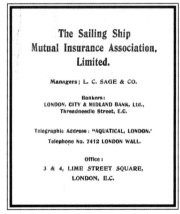

Sailing Ship Mutual Insurance
Association Booklet c. 1906

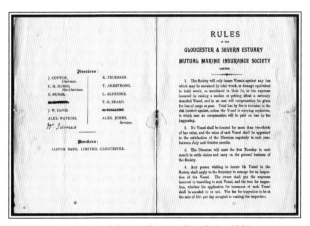

Gloucester & Severn Estuary Club Rules 1904

[6] Takadata Imaizumi, 'Transition of Shipowners' Liability Laws and Changes of P & I Clubs in the UK (Part 1)' *Yokohama Business Review*, Vol. X, No. 3 (1989), pp. 221-241

[7] Sailing Ship Mutual Association List of Entered Vessels
[8] Steamship Mutual Articles of Association

Sailing Ship was established in 1906 in the same year that the Workmen's Compensation Act (WCA) extended employers' liabilities to seamen and the first list of ships shows just 126 ships entered by 49 shipowners. The ships were small wooden sailing vessels (less than 300 tons) and were mainly engaged in the British coastal trade and it is difficult to ascertain the total tonnage as few of the ships appear in *Lloyd's Register* as many were under the 100 ton limit for Lloyd's. An early circular in 1907 claimed a contributing capital of just under £500,000. The main predecessor to Sailing Ship was a small club based in Gloucester in the West of England. Forty one of the vessels appear in a list of ships entered with Gloucester & Severn Estuary Mutual Insurance Society Ltd in 1904 to 1906. The secretary was Alexander Johns and Charles Nurse was the vice chairman. This mainly local club insured vessels owned along the coast between Bridgwater and Cardiff, although there were exceptions such as the *Charlotte Kilner* of Hull and *Tankerton Tower* of Whitstable. It was a hull club and insured vessels for two–thirds of their value — the average full value of the vessels was £500.[9] These vessels were seen as higher risk by the established P&I Clubs many of whom by now were predominately steam. So with increased liabilities from the WCA in 1906 Johns and Nurse combined with Sage and others to set up a specific club for sailing vessels.

The Coastal Sailing Ship

Albert Westcott was amongst the very first owners to join the Sailing Ship Mutual and was, from the beginning, an active member of the Sailing Ship Committee. Albert at the time had three ships entered in his name but took over the family fleet of ships when his father, John, died in 1913. It was said of Albert that he was devoted to his schooners and this strong loyalty to the wooden sailing vessel was not untypical.[10] Many still felt that a ship for which the motive power was free still had a place alongside the steamship. The sailing ship remained a key factor in the early years and their owners were a dedicated if stubbornly loyal group of men.

Chart 1 : Sailing Ship owner locations, 1908
(from list of entered vessels, Lloyd's Register and Mercantile Navy List)

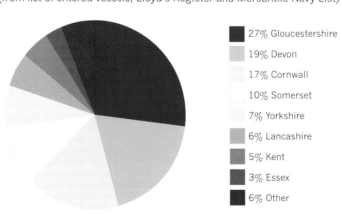

27% Gloucestershire
19% Devon
17% Cornwall
10% Somerset
7% Yorkshire
6% Lancashire
5% Kent
3% Essex
6% Other

The names of the owners and their ships entered into the Sailing Ship Association in 1908 read like a *Who's Who* of famous sailing ships and men. The South West of England was well represented. The counties of Gloucestershire, Devon, Cornwall and Somerset accounted for 73 per cent of the entered tonnage (see Chart 1). There were Alexander Johns and the Nurse brothers already mentioned who were based in Gloucester with 28 ships between them, Edward Hamblin of Bridgwater with five ships, Edward Stephens of Charlestown had entered his fleet of eleven ships and William Varcoe Kellow of Par had five ships. The other large fleet was that of Thomas Ashburner of Barrow, who had nine ships. There were several single ships entered and in many cases these vessels were owned by the master, such as John Raddings of Goole with his ship *Charlotte Kilner* and G Millington of Liverpool with *Water Bird*. The *Tankerton Tower*, owned by H Haddon was from Whitstable and was the first of many that would come from that port. Only a third of the 189 vessels appear in *Lloyd's Register*. They were mainly in the 120 ton range with the smallest being Chichester's 37 ton *Rosita* and the largest the 296 ton *E S Hocken* of Fowey owned and managed by John Edward Hocken. The oldest ship was built in 1840 and was owned by Nurse and almost all the other ships were built before 1900. The average year of building was 1873, which was a peak period for wooden sailing ship building in Britain.

Most of the sailing ships were built for very different trades to those in which they were now engaged. Alexander Johns owned the 145 ton *Esmeralda*, built in Brixham in 1860 a wooden three-masted schooner built for the fruit trade and another fruit schooner was the *Rhoda Mary*. Fruit schooners were not the so called clippers (a rather specialised and often misused term), but were small, fine lined vessels, built for speed. They were able to compete effectively with steam until the 1880s by bringing back small consignments of fruit from the Azores and the West Indies to the winter markets in London and Bristol.[11] Now even that trade was closed to them and they were, like many others, working in the coastal trade carrying low value high volume goods such as coal and china clay. Speed was no longer required, just cheap transport.

In 1906 there were still 4,500 sailing ships on the British registers, totalling over 1.3 million tons and employing over 24,000 men, of whom about 6,000 were foreigners. Of these sailing vessels, 86 per cent were less than 400 tons and employed 47 per cent of the men in the sailing ship trades. The overwhelming majority of these sailing ships were now restricted solely to the coastal trades.[12] The coastal trade had expanded up to 1914 and was at its zenith. Virtually all ports were linked by a dense network of coastal liners that provided a fast and regular scheduled service, but this was not what these ships were doing. These sailing ships and barges were in the minority, the sailing ship by 1900 was just one eighth of the tonnage of entries in coastal trade. Compared to steam the sailing ship was unreliable, it depended on wind strength and was affected by currents and tides and could spend days in port through adverse weather conditions. Its main advantage was

[9] Gloucester & Severn Estuary Mutual Insurance Society Ltd Rule book

[10] Ian Merry, *The Westcotts and their Times*, (National Maritime Museum; 1977), p. 17

[11] Helen Doe, *Jane Slade of Polruan*, (Truran, 2001)

[12] British Parliamentary Papers (1907): Annual Statement of the Navigation and Shipping of the United Kingdom for 1906

E S Hocken, 296-ton barquentine, managing owner J E Hocken, Fowey

its 'provision of a very cheap form of bulk transport – a floating warehouse, cheaper than other forms of coaster and all modes of land transport'. Schooners of 100 registered tons could carry about 160 tons of goods with a crew of three. Improvements in rig design and the use of winches and self-furling gear increased. Coal was the largest commodity carried by coastal ship, amounting to 20.5 million tons by 1913.[13]

For bulky goods whose unit value was low, which did not deteriorate and which were not needed at a particular date, the sailing coaster offered the cheapest form of transport. Thus sand, stone, ballast, manure and grains were normal cargoes. In addition those goods which required careful and therefore lengthy loading usually went by sailing ship, for the demurrage costs were much lower in sail than steam because the latter's original capital cost was so much greater. In the early twentieth century, goods like slates which cracked easily, bricks which were prone to chipping, and tiles and fireclay: products which were frangible tended to be transported in sailing coasters.[14]

Management of the Club

The early members of Sailing Ship were highly experienced shipowners and master mariners, and in many cases such as Nurse and Johns, also had club management experience. The first Chairman, Charles Nurse, was typical. He had gone to sea at an early age and become a master mariner. In the early 1890s together with his brother Frank, he set up a coastal shipping business based at Gloucester. By 1910 he had retired from active sea-going life and concentrated on running the business which included acting as shipbroker. Charles Nurse continued running the C & F Nurse Brothers Shipping Company until March 1913, when he died. The company was dissolved and all his coasting vessels sold off.[15]

Allowing for the normal neutral tone of official minutes of meeting the early Committee meetings of Sailing Ship Mutual appear to have been lively ones. By 1910 the meetings were now being held at 49 Leadenhall Street, which was the office of the firm of W & W Stocken. The first balance sheet that can be traced shows the position for Classes 4 and 5 (the P&I Classes) as at 20th February 1909. Claims and expenses for that year, including the balance from earlier years, amounted to £5,559 3s 2d of which Committee expenses were £152 10s 4d. The bank balance was £342.

At the Annual General Meeting in 1910 Charles Nurse was in the chair. Finances were agreed and claims were discussed in detail. The Rules were discussed at 'some length' and it would seem no agreement was reached so the issue was deferred to the Committee. By late 1910, 550 vessels were entered in Classes 4 and 5 and in December a circular stated the contributing capital as £504,780. The average cost of a vessel entered in the Association for Protection, Indemnity and Defence was three shillings (fifteen pence) per ton, or for a vessel of 40 tons it was £6 and for a vessel of 80 tons it was £12. For vessels not requiring Indemnity or Defence cover the cost would be £4 10s and £9 respectively.

The figure of 3s per ton was based on one of the worst years the Association had encountered at that stage. For the first ten months of the 1910/11 underwriting year the call would have been less than 1s 6d (seven and a half pence) per ton, making the cost for a vessel of 40 tons £3 and a vessel of 80 tons £6. In November and December 1910 there were exceptionally heavy gales – even worse than those of the previous year – across the Irish Sea and Bristol Channel. The *Charlotte Kilner* incurred a general average claim when carrying a cargo of salt fish from Hull to Exeter; the vessel had to sacrifice its anchor and chain and then head to Lowestoft for repair.[16] One case under the Workmen's Compensation Act arose from the total loss of the three-masted schooner *Lucy Johns*. This prompted an 'on account payment' of £700. This loss was a particular tragedy for Charles Nurse as his brother Frank was the master of the *Lucy Johns* and the ship had been lost with all hands.

[13] John Armstrong, 'Climax and Climacteric:
   The British Coastal Trade, 1870–1930', p. 37
[14] Armstrong, 'British Coastal Trade', p. 46

[15] Jonathan Seagrove correspondence 20th August 2008
[16] David Raddings collection: Documents relating to
   General Average *Charlotte Kilner*

By 1911 at the next Annual General Meeting Albert Westcott was in the chair when the issue of barges was raised. Already there were perceived differences in risk between the sailing shipowners and the barge owners and 'It was decided that the committee should separate the risk between flat bottomed vessels and round. If necessary another Association be registered with the name Barge appearing in it'.[17] This debate continued at the next two Committee meetings at which Alfred Stocken now appeared beside Lionel Sage. In May 1912 it was agreed to set up the Thames Estuary and Coasting Sailing Barge Mutual Insurance and Protection Association Limited, thus separating barge and sail. Barges worked mainly in shallow coastal areas and in river estuaries, their flat bottoms allowing them to beach easily. In the 1908 ships list there are Tamar barges, Thames barges and Gloucester trows, all vessels specifically designed for their rivers and estuaries, but the new club had a distinctly South East bias in its representation. Lionel Sage was named as the manager and the other subscribers on the legal document setting up the new club were E A Hibbs of Brightlingsea barge owner, Clement W Parker of Bardwell on Sea barge owner, A A Hutson of Maidstone barge owner, H Shrubsall East Greenwich barge builder, E Baigent and Walter Howard of Water Lane EC shipbrokers, and Percy Hitchcock, Richmond, clerk.

The management of the Association continued to develop. Sailing Ship was the largest of the three associated clubs and the Committee increased its scrutiny in June 1912 requesting that the Managers should furnish the Committee with a list of vessels at risk

Captain Raddings, on the right, and the crew of the *Charlotte Kilner*

Youngarth, an example of a typical spritsail barge. This one was owned by Portland Cement and is pictured in Southampton in 1939.

and to inform subsequent meetings of new entries. The issue of part-time management arose as Lionel Sage was managing the Association as part of his brokerage business and Alfred Stocken had his own legal practice. With three Clubs, Sailing Ship, Steamship and Thames Estuary as part of the Association, the business was more complex, although the major business was all done through Sailing Ship. By the 1912 Annual General Meeting 'the question of employing a permanent manager' was discussed and the Committee were authorised to 'make such arrangements as they deemed necessary'.[18]

The Committee business shows the close involvement of the Committee members in individual cases. For example there was the case of the total loss of the *Rosa V* where the member in this case had not paid his premiums. This led to what is described as a 'Full discussion' with two members, Captain L Nurse and Parker, proposing it be disallowed while an amendment by Albert Westcott and Captain Charles Nurse proposed that it be deferred and that the member, Mr Wilson, be asked to attend a meeting.[19] Wilson duly attended the Committee meeting two months later to explain his case in person. 'After a very full examination of Mr Wilson and the fullest discussion' it was proposed by Daniels and seconded by Westcott that an '*in gratis* payment be made'. £200 was proposed and the claim was eventually settled at £150. It was not just owners who were called before the Committee. In January 1914 the master of the *Mary Ann*, Captain Jarman, attended and was examined by the Committee in reference to the loss of his vessel on the Gunfleet Sand. Subsequently the Managers were asked to notify the Committee of changes in masters. An interesting concept today for the Committee but possible in a club where the number of entered ships was less than 600.

Full use of the expertise of the Committee members was made. In June 1912 the question of appointing a permanent surveyor for the Association was discussed, but it was decided to 'leave as at present'. So in the case of the salvage of the *Gladys* the managers were empowered to settle up to £75 and one of the Committee members, Mr Hibbs, was sent to Lowestoft to try to settle it. Albert Westcott was a marine surveyor as well as a shipowner and when in November 1913 the *Speedwell* claimed to be damaged at Plymouth, Westcott examined the vessel, but found no damage. In the case of the *Elinor* at Milford, Captain L Nurse, based at Bridgwater, was requested to undertake a survey.

Promotion of the Club

From an early stage the newly formed Sailing Ship Association set out to increase its tonnage and Lionel Sage was very active in writing to prospective members in order to achieve this aim. A simple booklet explained the advantages of the new Association and it was sent in 1907 to 'all owners taken from the 1907 Mercantile List'. One can only assume it was sent to all coastal sailing shipowners. The main selling points were:

[17] Sailing Ship AGM 18th April 1911
[18] Sailing Ship AGM 30th May 1912
[19] Sailing Ship Committee Meeting 15th Nov 1912

The association has agents in most of the principal ports enabling Captains who require advice to obtain same speedily. The fact that the Protection Club affords the benefits of a Legal or Defence Club disposes of the necessity of owners entering another Club for the protection usually afforded by such Clubs is a great convenience. The Committee are gentlemen of considerable experience and appreciate the requirements arising out of the ownership of coasting vessels[20]

Just a few months earlier in November 1906, Sage had written a circular to members claiming the success of the new Club.

Dear Sir,
As members are aware, previous to the formation of this Association, the managers of other Associations and certain shipowners unhesitatingly and emphatically stated that an Association, to be worked on the lines of this one, was undoubtedly doomed to failure and notwithstanding the opinion of such experienced shipowners composing our committee, numerous owners elected to defer joining until the Association had proved its own value.

Having regard to this, the Committee have thought it advisable to issue a call sheet from which owners will have the opportunity of seeing for themselves that the views of the committee have been justified and that an association such as ours is destined to work out very much cheaper than others despite the extra benefit it affords to members.

L C Sage, managers [21]

By April 1910 the Club was pushing for more members. Letters were sent to insurance brokers enclosing entry forms and posters outlining the range of rates. With regard to Class 6 it was pointed out that a Captain, as well as an owner, could insure against loss

A W Daniels, Whitstable Club and Committee
member of Sailing Ship from 1912

of freight and effects arising out of the total loss of a vessel up to a maximum of £100. It was said that this was not possible with a local club. Owners in small local clubs were a particular target. Sage claimed that 'few if any of these clubs have sufficient capital or vessels to warrant them with prudence continuing business'. Owners had to wait longer for settlement of claims, had to pay for their defence of claims and were under insured. Small clubs were often under funded and, with a small number of members, risks were not spread well in the face of increasing complexity and legislation. The local clubs that were a particular target were the Padstow and Newquay clubs in Cornwall and the Dee and Port Madoc clubs in North Wales.[22]

The tactic of targeting the small clubs paid off and the gradual expansion of the Association continued and in November 1912 it was announced that the Whitstable club had been taken over and Messrs A W Daniels, J G Gann and A Anderson were elected to serve on the Committee. All of these men were involved in the coal trade and their vessels, many bought cheaply from other ports, were operated by the most basic of crew in what was known in its time as a hard and difficult trade.[23] This was the start of Abbie Anderson's long association with Sailing Ship Mutual.

The target market for Steamship was also very specific. The first surviving letter with Steamship on the letter heading was written in January 1913 by Lionel Sage. The heading was 'The Steamship Mutual Underwriting Association Ltd for Coastal Vessels' and the letter drew attention to the advantage that the 'steamships in this Association contribute on a minimum tonnage of 150 tons being considerably less than the minimum basis in other Associations'. The handwritten note beside it shows it was sent to 'Holmans, Ness[sic] and North of England owners.'[24]

A few weeks later another letter was sent out, this time to the Padstow, Newquay and Dee clubs showing the advantages of the Sailing Ship Association. A further letter sent in October of the same year to the small clubs highlighted the disastrous losses

> *...that members of local clubs have suffered in the last few years which in some cases have led to calls of over 20 per cent per annum being made, we would advise all owners to carefully consider the question of whether it would not be better for them to enter a strong Association and thus do away with the possibility of incurring a responsibility which might be serious and at the same time know that the Association in which they are entered is legally constituted and the liability of its members limited.*

> *The section of this Association which takes Hull risks has over 400 vessels entered and the contributing capital is just under £200,000 making it by far the largest of its kind in the Kingdom. Vessels can be entered at any time and the fullest details will be given on application.*[25]

[20] Sailing Ship Circulars Book
[21] Sailing Ship Circulars Book
[22] Sailing Ship Circulars Book

[23] Basil Greenhill, *Merchant Schooners*, (London; Conway Maritime Press, 1988), pp. 170-172
[24] Sailing Ship Circulars Book
[25] Sailing Ship Circulars Book

First World War

The First World War saw the Association based now at 49 Leadenhall Street where they had been since 1911. W & W Stocken had also moved there. L C Sage and Company were still listed as the managers and the telegraphic address was still 'Aquatical' (a word now retained as the name of Steamship Mutual's office in London).

War losses did not just come from enemy action. In 1907 John Raddings purchased the 70 ton schooner *Charlotte Kilner* from his father for the sum of £450. John used his savings of £100 and took out a mortgage for the rest. The vessel had been built in 1882 in Goole, near Hull on the North East Coast of England. This he then sailed with a small crew of three, working around the coast and eventually paying off the mortgage in 1909. He continued trading through the war and in December 1916 he loaded stone from Alderney in the Channel Islands for Grimsby. Just six days later they were waiting off Grimsby for a tug, which was required for navigating the boom under Admiralty wartime regulations. The next day the tug was alongside but due to blackout regulations there was no anchor light and in the dark the minesweeper *Valmont* collided with her. The stone cargo resulted in the *Charlotte Kilner* sinking rapidly, the crew were saved by the tug but the vessel was a total loss.[26] An urgent telegram to Sailing Ship Mutual received a reply from Sage with the request that Raddings should visit a named local solicitor 'at once' and requesting details of the cargo owners and their underwriters. A letter from Sage to Raddings ten days later acknowledged receipt of the report made by Raddings to the Admiralty with the comment 'We think it is a pity you made any report to them at all'.[27] Not surprisingly the Committee meeting in January 1917 unanimously agreed to proceed with action against the Admiralty who promptly rejected the claim.[28] Meanwhile Raddings needed a livelihood and purchased the *Princess* for £1,000. This was then lost with all hands on 22nd March 1917 having set sail for Guernsey. Mrs Raddings now had to handle the correspondence with Sage and Stocken. A payment of £1,000 was made for the loss of *Princess* and the Admiralty was persuaded to pay up for the *Charlotte Kilner*.[29]

Ships were requisitioned by the Admiralty for a range of duties and one of these was to be a 'Q' ship or 'Mystery' ship. The *Record Reign* was a ketch registered at Maldon, Essex.

Cumberland Lassie, three-masted topsail schooner of Folkestone, lost in 1917

Princess, ketch registered in Goole, lost with all hands 1917

In 1915 the Admiralty converted her to a Q ship. Two diesel engines were installed and the vessel was armed with four small guns and one large gun, the latter being hidden under a dummy ship's boat. These Q ships, with naval gun crews aboard, would resemble in every respect the type of small coasting sailing vessel plying the coast. Enemy submarine commanders would typically prefer to surface, force the vessel to stop and sink her by gunfire rather than waste an expensive torpedo on a vessel of less than 2,000 tons. When the submarine surfaced the Q ship would appear to comply with orders to stop and abandon ship. Once in range Royal Navy colours would be hoisted, hidden guns cleared for action and the submarine engaged.[30] Another Q ship entered with Sailing Ship Mutual was the *Result*, a schooner from Barrow, which was owned then by H G G Clarke of Braunton.[31] It was taken over by the Admiralty and armed and fitted with a 45 horse-power motor.[32] Both the *Result* and the *Record Reign* survived the war and the latter was eventually lost in thick fog off the coast of Devon with a cargo of coal on the morning of 8th February 1935. The claim was settled for £495.

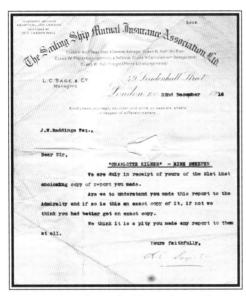

Letter from Sage to Raddings reference the sinking of *Charlotte Kilner*, 1916

Charlotte Kilner, 80-ton ketch, owner J W Raddings of Hull

26 http://www.pilotmag.co.uk/2008/06/30/to-be-a-pilot-the-story-behind-a-painting/

27 David Raddings correspondence September 2008

28 Sailing Ship Minutes January 1917

29 Sailing Ship Minutes March 1917; David Raddings correspondence

30 G H and R Bennett, 'Maritime Cornwall in the Era of Two World Wars' in Doe, et al (eds) *Maritime History of Cornwall*, (University of Exeter Press; forthcoming 2010)

31 Sailing Ship Mutual insurance certificate in Robert D'Arcy Andrews, *Braunton, Home of the Last Sailing Coasters*, (Braunton: Braunton & District Museum, 2007), p. 41

32 Tim Latham, *Ashburner Schooners*, (Ready Rhino Publications; 1991), p. 119; Greenhill, *Merchant Schooners*, pp. 193-94

Result in 1953, passing inside the Longship's lighthouse off Lands End, a route only taken by experienced sailors

At a Committee meeting on 28th January 1916 the death of Captain Charles Nurse was reported. Lionel Sage referred to his membership 'since the incorporation of the Association and his indefatigable work on behalf of the Association'. Charles Nurse had been present at a Committee meeting just six months before. At the same meeting the 'committee requested Mr Sage to write to Mr Stocken to express their concern at his illness and to wish him a speedy recovery'.[33] He did recover and became more firmly involved with the Club in July 1917 when he took over from Sage as Manager and Sage became Secretary.

Stocken's closer involvement was evident in his negotiations with the Government regarding war risks. The losses were too heavy for the Club to manage and on 16th August 1917 the Coasting Vessels Mutual War Risks Association Limited was set up with reinsurance by the Government. Not all losses were war related and some were expensive. The *Punta Ninfa* was a steel three-masted schooner of 383 tons built in 1898 and was purchased from Argentinian owners in 1917. She sailed from Buenos Aires for the coast of France and then on passage from Le Havre to Cardiff, went ashore, and was a total loss; all the crew were saved.[34] She had presumably been purchased to take advantage of the shortage of ships and the rising war time needs for freight to France. In the same year the *Cumberland Lassie* was also lost. Both claims came to £4,000.

At the Annual General Meeting of Sailing Ship on 28th May 1918, it was announced that Lionel Sage, age 36, had resigned from the 'Management of the Company'. No reason was given and perhaps he became involved with war work. He had been with the Association since the outset and had been instrumental in developing much of the business. The Chairman paid tribute to the work he had done.[35] Sage remained in insurance and was listed post-war in the 1920 London directory as

> *Lionel Sage and Company Ltd, Steamship and insurance broker, 5 Fenchurch Street EC3 TN Avenue 2359 (Lloyds EC3 and Baltic EC3)* [36]

Sage prospered and was present in 1933 at a reception given by Lloyd's to delegates to the Monetary and Economic Conference in London at which Prince George and several Cabinet ministers were also present.[37]

Meanwhile in 1918 Alfred Stocken was left with a job to fill and he had to manage for the rest of the war on his own while also running his legal practice. As for the shipowners, they needed to consider the after effects of the conflict and optimism was high as they anticipated a post-war increase in freight rates and a return to pre-war activity. But for the coastal sailing ships the picture did not look good.

[33] *Sailing Ship Minutes* 28th January 1916
[34] *Lloyd's Register* 1916-17
[35] David Hooper, *Steamship History* (draft), p. 27
[36] *Kelly's Post Office Directory* 1920
[37] *The Times* 23rd June 1933

Chapter 2

THE INTER WAR YEARS

Despite the conservatism of Abbie Anderson, the long serving Chairman who dominated the Committee throughout the inter war years, and the reservations of Alfred Stocken, the first seeds of internationalism are sown with the arrival of Sydney Crowe and these foreshadow the greater changes to come.

Background

The war had a major impact on the coastal trade with the loss of ships by enemy action, the switching of goods to rail for safety, ships requisitioned by the Government for the carriage of troops, munitions, pit props for the trenches and coal, plus deployment as the famous Q ships. The coastal trade did not recover to pre-war levels and by 1922 coastal activity was less than three quarters of that achieved in 1913.[1]

One cause cited by shipowners for the post-war difficulties was competition from Dutch motor coasters and the Dutch were blamed in several sources, notably in those relating to Thames barges many of which were insured within the Sailing Ship Mutual Association. This was not in fact the case as the overall market share of the Dutch was relatively small and the problem of the coastal trade was one of overall relative decline. Coal had been the major pre-war cargo, but this freight decreased by 30 per cent in the post-war years and the overall market for coal was in decline as oil became more popular. The over supply of coasters forced down freight rates, wages were 80 per cent higher than before the war and there was increased competition from the railways which were still subsidised by the Government. For the sailing ships this was in many cases to be their death knell. The coastal fleet response to these factors was slow but one aspect was increased mergers and adoption of new technology such as diesel. The number of coastal tankers increased from 800 registered tons in 1914 to 5,000 by 1929.[2] The sailing ship was out of place and out of time although the sailing barge still managed to cling on, supported by strong local traditions in places such as the Thames and Medway.

In June 1919 the Sailing Ship Mutual Committee meeting for Classes 4 and 5 was attended by seven members and chaired by Albert Westcott. Also present was Alfred Stocken and for the first time John Plincke. Plincke was known to Stocken and had been a shipbroker before the war. He had served in Mesopotamia and by February 1919 was in Salonika waiting to be released from the army. Demobilisation of the armed forces was not a fast task and so Stocken wrote in April to the Military Secretary at the War Office to speed up Plincke's release and carefully aligned the request to Government needs.

We should be obliged if it is possible if Captain Plincke could be demobilised at the earliest possible moment as we are most anxious to have his services in connection with many important insurance matters and to get out certain statistics for us required by Government offices which have had to be delayed during the last two or three years owing to the inefficiency of our staff due to a great number of them joining the Army.[3]

Plincke disembarked in Southampton on 6th April and was at the Committee meeting in Leadenhall Street barely two months later to fill the gap left by Lionel Sage.[4]

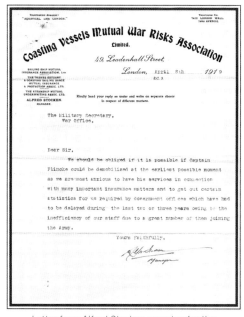

Letter from Alfred Stocken pressing for the
early release of John Plincke, 1919

John Frederick Plincke,
Secretary of Sailing Ship from 1919

[1] Armstrong, 'Coastal Trade', pp. 46-47
[2] Armstrong, 'Coastal Trade', pp. 48-54
[3] R Plincke: Letter A S Stocken to War Office 8th April 1919
[4] R Plincke: War Office Arrival Report dated 28th April 1919

Expansion

In September 1919 the quest for tonnage was renewed with a circular, which was sent to members of all Clubs. The circular outlined the advantages and listed the ports for rating purposes and all of the ports mentioned were within the bounds of the British Home Trade. The rates quoted ranged from the 'Clyde and South thereof, North of Mersey to the North coast of Devon and Cornwall' 5s per cent (£0.25) to West coast of France to Holland 22s 6d per cent (£1.125). The cost of covering freight against war risks varied from 1s per cent (£0.05) to 1s 6d per cent (£0.075).[5]

The emphasis was still firmly on the British coastal trade. Despite war depredations there was still a view that this market was worth pursuing. When the Chamber of Shipping formed a separate section for coasting vessels in 1920 it was estimated that there were well over 1,000 belonging to some 600 owners registered at small ports around the coast.[6]

The situation for the remaining coastal sail was difficult and increasingly bleak and in 1919 an initiative to form a Shipowners' Association as a lobbying group came from Sailing Ship Mutual. Discussions had been held in 1918 with the Chamber of Shipping and although some progress was made at that time, the formation of this Association had been deferred. At the Annual General Meeting of Sailing Ship Mutual on 2nd April 1919 a decision was taken to go ahead with the project. It was proposed that the organisation be called the Coasting Sailing Ship Owners' Association Ltd. A circular headed with the name of the proposed group (and sub-headed 'For the protection of the interests of Owners of Sailing, Fishing, Motor or Auxiliary Vessels') was sent out explaining that the intention of the Association was to achieve unity among the owners of coasting sailing ships in order

Albert Westcott, Sailing Ship Committee member
from 1906 and Chairman

to protect them and to safeguard their interests. The letter to owners said that there were numerous matters that solely affected owners of coasting sailing ships, such as particularly onerous conditions in charter parties, which a unified approach from owners might succeed in having omitted, or at least altered. Many charter parties contained terms imposing charges on the owners which were wholly unfair, as well as an obligation on the crew to load and discharge cargoes. Another issue requiring change was the prevailing custom of sailing vessels being detained during loading and discharge, while steamers arriving after the sailing vessel were given priority for these services. With unity amongst owners and an Association supporting them, it was felt that these 'injustices' could be remedied.[7]

The plan was that the intended pressure group, the Shipowners' Association, (not to be confused with the Mutual Club of the same name) would be associated in some way with the Chamber of Shipping, but would be independent of the P&I Clubs. It was signed by Alfred Stocken as pro-tem Secretary. After this circular there are no further details of the fate of this Association but evidently some progress was made as the charter party issue was subsequently handled by the Documentary Committee of the Chamber of Shipping.

Eighteen insurance associations signed up to the proposed regulations and committed their members to complying with the list of approved charter parties with some strong words of warning:

> It is strictly required…that no alterations…be made in the documents and members are warned that…to consent to any alteration…is a breach of the Rules…which renders Members liable to the consequences prescribed. These are of a serious and drastic nature and may result in the Member being deprived of the cover afforded by the Associations.

> British Marine Mutual Insurance Association Limited
> British Steamship Short Trades Association
> British Steamship Owners Association
> Britannia Steamship Insurance Association
> Clyde Steamship Insurance Association Limited
> Hull Mutual Steam Ship Protecting Society Limited
> London Steamship Owners Mutual Insurance Association Limited
> Neptune Steamship Protecting and Indemnity Association
> Newcastle Protection and Indemnity Association
> North of England Protecting and Indemnity Association
> Sailing Ship Mutual Insurance Association Limited
> Standard Steamship Owners' Protection and Indemnity Association
> Standard Ship Owners' Freight, Dead Freight, Demurrage & Defence Association Limited

[5] Sailing Ship Circulars Book
[6] S Crowe, SSM Club History Notes, undated
[7] Hooper, Steamship History (draft)

Sunderland Steamship Protecting and Indemnity Association Limited
United Kingdom Freight, Demurrage & Defence Association
United Kingdom Mutual Steamship Assurance Association Limited
United Shipowners Freight, Demurrage & Protective Association, Limited
West of England Steamship Owners' Protection and Indemnity Association Limited [8]

Trying to assist and encourage members in the use of sensible contracts was evident from a letter, dated 10th May 1924, containing an eight page list of compulsory charter parties. This was sent to H H Poole & Co Ltd, F B Cooper, A B Clarks, McNabb Mougier & Co (Italy) Ltd, Wm Thomas & Sons, Matthew & Luff, Millonic & Goulder, Hannan Samuel & Co, Chase S/S Co Ltd and R & W Paul Ltd. Many of these members were small locally based companies in small ports. Further conformity came about on 1st January 1925 when the Carriage of Goods by Sea Act, 1924, came into force requiring that every Bill of Lading or similar document of title issued in Great Britain or Northern Ireland had to have an express statement that it was subject to the provisions of Rules as applied by the Act. [9]

It is in 1923 that there were some related incidents within the Committee that suggest a struggle for influence. From inception the person acting as Chairman had changed every year and now Abbie Anderson was in the chair. Albert Westcott had served before as Chairman and had been with the Club since it began. The first dispute arose over a new rule relating to the Common Carriers Clause. Westcott had attempted to delay its implementation and at the next meeting in March 1925 he moved that the minutes of the previous meeting were not in order. This motion was not seconded and it is not clear what the difficulty was. Shortly afterwards Westcott became involved in another dispute with the Committee in relation to his 140 ton steel schooner, *Rothersand*. The vessel, built in Germany in 1907, had been owned by Westcott for just three years. In June the case of the *Rothersand* (damage received during dry-docking) was discussed. The Chairman, Abbie Anderson, proposed that the case should not be contested and this was carried. However after further discussion it was agreed to discuss the issue again at the next meeting. Westcott, unhappy with this decision, then raised the question again after several members of the Committee had left and the remaining Committee members refused to deal with it, but suggested that 'he could raise it at the next Meeting if he deemed fit'. The case duly came up at the next meeting and the original agreement, not to contest it, was confirmed. [10]

In June 1925 it is not surprising that Albert Westcott decided not to offer himself for re-election at the Annual General Meeting. He had been a member of the Sailing Ship Mutual since its incorporation, a Committee member since January 1911 and had frequently been a chairman of the Committee. The rather oddly worded sentence in the minutes hints of strong views expressed. 'The manager moved an expression of regret at Mr. Westcott's refusal to offer himself for re election.' [11] Albert died aged 59 in 1936 and his obituary in the Plymouth newspaper reflected his long career in shipowning and that he had 'carried on the business until the slump some years ago'. In the early 1930s as freight rates dropped to uneconomic levels even for sailing ships he disposed of his ships and invested in property in Plymouth. His son later recalled him as a man of remarkable energy. [12]

Rothersand, schooner owned by
Albert Westcott, Plymouth

The significance of the departure of Albert Westcott was that it heralded the unchallenged reign of Abbie Anderson as the Club's longest serving Chairman. Anderson was a Director of Anderson, Rigden and Perkins, based in Whitstable, Kent which built wooden barges. His knowledge and experience was of the coastal trade in the South East of England and from this time the emphasis of the Club moved from the South West of England.

Economic Problems

The difficult economic situation placed strains on many owners and the Clubs recognised this with a circular issued by Sailing Ship and Steamship Mutual on 30th June 1922, which said that the funds of the Association were such that the Committee felt able to relieve members of the liability to pay the next quarter's instalment due on 20th August. The Committee appreciated the difficulties owners were having to contend with and it was hoped that when the November quarterly instalment became due the Committee would be able to certainly reduce the amount of the instalment, if not waive it altogether. In fact, when the November instalment became due, it was reduced by fifty per cent. Furthermore, three months later it was announced that the quarterly instalments would be reduced from 6d per ton per class to 4d per ton per class.[13]

8 Sailing Ship Circulars Book
9 Hooper, Steamship History (draft)
10 Sailing Ship Minutes March to June 1925
11 Sailing Ship Minutes June 1925

12 *Merry, The Westcotts and their Times*, p. 17
13 Sailing Ship Circulars Book; Minutes 10th February 1923

Bessie Ellen, 87-ton ketch built in 1904 in Plymouth and still operating out of Plymouth

Management of Committees

During the 1920s the meetings of the various committees were rationalised. The first action was to coordinate dates so that they did not conflict with the British Sailing Ship Owners Association to which several Committee members belonged.[14] The next action was to reduce the number of Committee members in Sailing Ship for Classes 1, 2 and 6. In March 1923 it was proposed by Westcott that the Sailing Ship Committee be reduced to just four people and the Finance Committee meetings were further reduced to just two meetings per year and they required the attendance of just one Committee member. By 1925 Abbie Anderson proposed the reduction to just three members and more claims were referred to the discretion of the Managers. The hull business was declining. For P&I (Classes 4 and 5) the Committee was nine men and this was reduced to eight in June 1920. Abbie Anderson's name appears constantly as Chairman of both Committees and by March 1929 it was agreed that just one member of Committee could sign cheques.[15] Anderson had now consolidated his influence over the Association.

Two claims illustrate the type of business going through Sailing Ship Mutual's P&I Classes. In June 1920 came the death of Captain Jack Chichester of *Bessie Ellen*. He was a typical one man business, sailing with just two other crew in home waters. The *Bessie Ellen* was an 87 ton ketch built in Plymouth in 1904 and a twenty-five horse-power engine was fitted in 1916. The *Bessie Ellen* worked the coal trade from Lydney in Gloucestershire and Newport in Wales to Appledore, Devon and Lyme Regis in Dorset. Chichester died after falling over board and being crushed. Rather than sell the ship, his widow employed another master and continued to manage the *Bessie Ellen* until the end of the Second World War. The ship is still afloat and is now chartered out of Plymouth.[16]

The loss of the *Earl Cairns* came in 1929, due to a fire while in the Fal River. A Liverpool registered 127 ton schooner, she was bought by shipbrokers Toyne Carter and re-registered in Fowey in 1917 to take advantage of the cheap cost of such ships and the great need for ships during the war. In 1921 an auxiliary engine was added and according to the shipping registers she was 'A constructive loss by fire abandoned to the underwriters Sailing Ship Mutual Insurance Assn London 4 May 1929'.[17] At £2,065 she was one of the most serious claims in the 1930/31 underwriting year. She was not totally lost and was later used for barrage balloon anchorage duties in Falmouth during the Second World War.[18]

The first minute book relating to Steamship Mutual dates from 1924 and Mr R G Westcott of H H Poole of Ipswich (no relation to Albert Westcott) was elected Chairman. The minutes are brief and contain no details of financial matters or claims. Frequently there were just two or even one Committee member meeting with the Managers. By August 1927 Abbie Anderson was unanimously elected to serve on the Committee and he became Chairman of his third Club within the Group. The hull risks business for small coastal steamers was also declining and the active part of the Sailing Ship family of Clubs was all being done through Classes 4 and 5 of Sailing Ship Mutual. By 1930 when it was clear that values for hull risk were too high to be covered by a mutual club and the losses too heavy the hull risks section was abandoned.[19]

The barge business, or to give it its full name the Thames Estuary and Coasting and Sailing Barge Mutual Insurance and Protection Association Limited, continued almost unchanged. One of its biggest concerns was how to handle the insurance of barges fitted with 'auxiliary motor power and/or full motor power' and constant concern over values of barges. This was one Committee where Abbie Anderson was not present but he was closely linked to two key Committee members, Gann was his cousin and Daniels was from his home town of Whitstable. The Chairman was Horace Shrubsall, a noted barge builder from East Greenwich.[20]

The claims were often very small. The *Blanche* was a barge originally entered in 1920 with a value of £1,500 but this had been reduced to £700 by 1924 after a change in

[14] This may be the British Motor and Sailing Ship Owners Association

[15] Sailing Ship Minutes

[16] www.Bessie-Ellen.com; Andrews, *Braunton: Home of the Last Sailing Coasters*, p. 3

[17] Cornwall Record Office: MSR Fowey Shipping Registers

[18] Greenhill, *Merchant Schooners*, p. 114

[19] Crowe, SSM Club History Notes

[20] R H Perks, 'The Barge Builder-Horace Shrubsall of East Greenwich', *Bygone Kent*, Vol. 2 , No. 2 (1999), pp. 87-94

ownership. At the meeting in September 1926 a claim for £3 following the loss of an anchor and chain, for the cost of carrying the replacements from store to ship, was considered. It was decided that this expense was not a claim under the policy, but in spite of this, the Committee agreed to the compromise offered by the Managers, which was £1.

The Committee hesitated in September 1933 when asked to approve a payment to the owner of £630 following the sinking of the barge. The hesitation arose from the fact that there was also a claim in the pipe-line for damage to the *Blanche* during loading. The Club needed confirmation that the damage had been repaired and did not therefore contribute to the sinking. After the vessel had been raised, it was inspected by H P Shrubsall (a famous name in Thames barge building), who confirmed that the sinking had in no way been caused by the loading damage. As a result, the settlement at £630 was approved. The final cost to the Club for this total loss was £640 2s 9d.

Rathbale, sailing barge, insured in 1909

Investment

In the early days of the Club claims could often be settled promptly but the increasing complexity, particularly of P&I claims, took rather longer and so there was a need to retain funds. The Committee for both sets of Classes agreed in December 1922 that a sum not exceeding £2,000 would be invested in 5 per cent War Loans in the names of A Anderson (Chairman), Captain L W Nurse and A Stocken 'as and when the managers feel the funds permit'. This is the first investment decision to emerge from the surviving records. In 1930 the Association's securities, including War Loans, were transferred to the Midland Bank to enable the bank to provide bail whenever the Association wanted to give security for a claim. In June 1933 the Managers were authorised to invest a further £1,500 in Government securities. It was later reported that £1,500 had been invested in 3 ½ per cent Australian stock. This, however, led to problems when in September it was disclosed that the transfer to Australian stock from 'Local Loans' had not taken place because the Chairman and Trustees were not in agreement. It was decided that the Trustees were not empowered to change the holding without the consent of the full Committee. The transfer did eventually happen and by November 1937, when the Australian loan was due to be repaid, the Trustees were authorised to invest the proceeds in such Trustee Securities as they thought fit.

Business Changes

P&I was now the main business of the Club and it was also providing reinsurance for two other clubs, the Sunderland Club and the Hull Mutual P&I Club. In 1934 Mr H G Clarke of the Braunton Shipowners' Association was elected to the Sailing Ship Committee for Classes 4 and 5 and this brought many Braunton ships into the Club. Braunton in North Devon had many of the last sailing schooners and ketches registered with its hull club, the Braunton Shipowners Mutual Marine Assurance Association and reinsurance was provided by Sailing Ship Mutual.[21]

Since the days of Lionel Sage and his letter writing, a new method of expanding business was tried by employing a member of staff to travel around the coast.

> One member of the staff, E R Howes, was the business getter. Each spring he left the office for three months and again for three months in the autumn. For each trip he received £250 for hotel and travelling expenses, giving no account for it and receiving neither more nor less wherever he went. Starting from Gravesend he went to all the ports where shipowners lived and there were dozens of them. Some that come to mind are Rochester, Whitstable, Margate, Ventnor, Fowey, Minehead, Connahs Quay and so on up to Wick (sometimes to Lerwick) and then down the east coast. He had neither car nor bicycle and received a commission on the business he

[21] Sailing Ship Minutes 1934; Andrews, *Braunton: Last Sailing Coasters*, pp. 2-14

brought, generally half the entrance fee on a ship which was two or three guineas. This was the only man ever so employed. He went to World War I in 1914 at the age of 17, spent three years in the trenches until wounded in 1917, came back to the City and worked as a traveller until he retired at 65 but still came to the office for a day or two a week until he died 10 years later.[22]

In 1928 there was another new initiative, the appointment of a foreign agent. A contract survives dated 21st December 1928, amended 1st August 1931, between Sailing Ship Mutual Insurance Association Limited and Noordelijk Assurantie Kantoor (The Northern Assurance Office Limited) of Groningen. It appoints NASK as sole agents for Holland and Germany to accept P&I entries and to sign insurance certificates. The authority was limited to vessels not exceeding 500 gross registered tons (grt). Liabilities covered included P&I, FD&D, removal of wreck, cargo liabilities, loss of life and personal injury, including persons on shore. Claims for liability for loss of life or personal injury to members of crew, workmen's compensation, four-fourths running down clause, and damage to fixed and floating objects were excluded. The rate of exchange for the tariff was one pound to 12 florins. The annual entrance fee varied from 1 grt to 100 grt £2 2s (£2.10) to 351 grt to 500 grt £5 5s (£5.25).

Arrival of Sydney Crowe

The minutes of a meeting on 13th June 1933 record for the first time the attendance of Sydney Crowe who was to play a major part in the development of the Association. He had been an average adjuster working for William Richards and Son, but clearly bright he caught the attention of Stocken and Plincke who persuaded him to move to the Sailing Ship Association in 1931 as a clerk. Crowe then went on to win one of two Institute of London Underwriters prizes on passing his Chartered Institute of Insurance exams (Marine Branch) in 1933.[23] He later recalled that the total staff including the partners was eight.

In the 1930's an office boy's weekly pay was 15 shillings (and ours came from New Malden in Surrey to get it) a typist's was £1 10s and a clerk's was £5. In spite of that, one typist worked with us from 1917 till she died nearly fifty years later and the filing clerk from the age of 15 to the age of 73 (though she had been begged to retire 10 years before that). The only bookkeeper worked on a high stool at a sloping desk for over forty years and never earned more than £22 a month until he died just after World War II. Stocken spent most of his time with his separate legal firm only emerging to attend Committee meetings. Committee meetings would horrify present day members. The Committee fees were two guineas a meeting (no one seemed to have expenses in those days whether they came from Bridgwater – as one did – or Glasgow) and there were 4 meetings a year. No agenda was sent out and the bulky memoranda of today was dispensed with. [24]

Crowe's view of Abbie Anderson who had been Chairman unopposed on all Committees since the departure of Albert Westcott is particularly telling:

The Chairman who reigned from 1911[sic] to 1950, was highly indignant when a newcomer suggested a change, would come in each Monday morning sign 20 blank cheques and depart to lunch and dominoes at Lake's in Eastcheap with Stocken and Plincke.[25]

His words reflect the very different business world of the inter war years and the small mutual insurance business he had joined. It was dominated still by men who remained loyal to the sailing ship and barge business. The arrival of Sydney Crowe, however, was to impact the Club significantly. His influence set in motion changes that would turn the Club from a small predominately English based organisation specialising in small coastal sailing vessels to an international Club covering ships of all sizes across the world and the early signs were evident before the Second World War.

In the same year that Crowe joined the Club the death was announced of another long term member. Theophilius William Couch came from Pentewan in Cornwall, one of the smallest ports in the South West. He was the last in a family of shipbrokers and managed the *Mary Miller*, *Polly & Emily* and *Conoid*. He had been a member throughout the war and a Committee member since 1920. In his place A F Struthers was appointed and his was to be another name that has a long association with the Club.

Sydney Crowe c. late 1930s

A F Struthers of J & A Gardner, Committee member from 1933 and Chairman

[22] Crowe, SSM Club History Notes
[23] Anthony Crowe; S R Crowe Letters and examination certificates, 1933

[24] Crowe, SSM Club History Notes
[25] Crowe, SSM Club History Notes

From Sail to Steam

In 1936 a landmark case arose. Among the remaining sailing vessels – ketches, brigantines, schooners and the like – entered with the Sailing Ship Club was the oldest ship on the books. The *Ceres* of Bude was built in 1811 in Salcombe and had served Wellington in the Peninsular War. She had been entered in 1906 and was to be lost off Croyde, North Devon in 1936. A payment of £802 was made.[26] The loss of the 125 year old vessel was reported widely, even as far away as Toronto, and she was described as the 'world's oldest ketch in active service, and the oldest vessel registered at Lloyd's'.[27]

Also in June 1936 a slight structural change took place. The minutes of Steamship with just Anderson for the Committee and Plincke and Crowe for the Managers saw detailed changes to the rules of Steamship. Twenty-five pages of minutes show that Steamship was now adopting all the Rules of Sailing Ship P&I. Steamship had come of age after being the junior partner for so long. Its establishment now seemed a farsighted pre-war decision, but loyalty to the Sailing Ship name was to keep that Association in the foreground for some time to come and Steamship claims continued to be discussed and noted in the Sailing Ship minutes. Another change was a name change, with the Thames Estuary Barge Association changing to the Coasting Vessels Mutual Marine Insurance Association Limited.

The resurrection of Steamship is indicative of the major change of direction that was occurring under the leadership of Sydney Crowe. The sailing ship and the coastal business was no longer sufficient, the Club now began to insure ocean going steamships.

> The largest vessel in the Steamship Mutual Club was of 690 tons gross. In 1936 two 505 gross tons coasters were entered owned by Mr Jack Billmeir who shortly afterwards became the chief supplier of ships to the Spanish Government then in exile in France. Billmeir rapidly enlarged his fleet to elderly 3-5,000 ton ships all of which he entered with the Club and the Managers had to re-organise their business methods to encompass the heavy reinsurance necessary. Other coasting owners joined in the lucrative business of carrying cargo to and from Republican Spain and when World War Two started in 1939 some 20 or 30 large ships up to 6,000 gross tons were entered.[28]

Sydney Crowe and Jack Billmeir were good friends and may have known each other for some years. They had much in common as they were both self made men who had left school at 14, then the conclusion of state education. They had started work in the City, Jack with a firm of shipbrokers and Sydney in average adjusting. They were much the same age and both were determined to make a good career out of shipping.

Ceres, two-man ketch rounding Barrel Rock, Bude in heavy weather

[26] Crowe, SSM Club History Notes; Sailing
   Ship Minutes
[27] *Toronto Times*, 12th December 1936
[28] Crowe, SSM Club History Notes

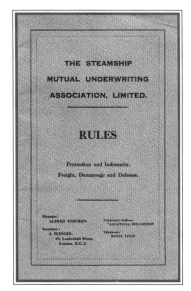

Steamship Mutual Rule Book c. 1930

Jack Billmeir and one of his masters, Captain Webster

Billmeir set out to accumulate capital and after finishing his daily work in the City he continued to work in the evenings and at weekends doing what he could to earn more money. His first investment was a £250 part interest in a ship, later progressing to a steam trawler in 1922 and an interest in an 8,000 ton steamer in 1924. These various ventures were not great successes. He became a member of the Baltic Exchange in 1927 and in 1931 formed his management company, J A Billmeir & Company Ltd, based in London. In 1934 he formed the shipowning company Stanhope Steamship Co Ltd with two steamers, *Stanhope* 505 tons and *Stanmore* 538 tons.[29] These two were insured with Steamship Mutual. With such small coasters, in his view there was no possibility of trading with the usual cargoes so he tried to find unusual ones. He delivered wine and timber which were normally carried in larger vessels but Billmeir delivered from the shipper direct to the merchant, carrying the cargo in his small vessels straight to their door.[30] But it was war that brought him his biggest opportunity.

Jack Billmeir and his ships became famous for their involvement in the Spanish Civil War. From two ships with a tonnage of 1,043 in 1936, he owned ten ships (16,958 tons) in 1937, and by 1938 the total was 21 ships (49,886 tons).[31] Some of these ships he owned for a very brief time, perhaps just one voyage to Spain and then they were sold with delivery at Marseille.[32] The British Government as part of the League of Nations had taken a neutral stance and questions were asked in Parliament about the ships, particularly Billmeir's. There were suspicions of gun running and his ships were searched on several occasions. Indeed in May 1938 the *Stancroft* was found to be carrying cartridge cases, aeroplane engines and other items as well as a general cargo. She was taken into Gibraltar where the master was charged. Billmeir sent Mr D Pritt, a senior barrister (and Member of Parliament) to argue the case. The master denied any knowledge and the Court decided there was no case to answer as the goods were being delivered from one part of the Spanish mainland to another.[33] Billmeir and his masters continued to take risks and his ships were constantly targeted by Franco's troops and their allies.

The *Standale* appears in the minutes in 1938. She had been abandoned off Lisbon and the crew of MV *Vandyck* had rendered very valuable services in rescuing the crew. As a consequence the Association had been saved a very large sum. The Committee of Lloyd's, the Board of Trade, and other 'Authorities had recognised these services and the Owner wished to join with the Association' in making some recognition on behalf of the *Standale*. A payment of £100 was agreed under Classes 4 and 5, with the owner contributing half.

The Civil War gave rise to a tremendous increase in shipments to Spain and corresponding claims. In 1937 a circular was sent to members requesting extra premiums for 'danger days' of 3s per crew member for each day in a Spanish port. In 1938 there were claims for injuries and medical expenses to crew on board *Stangrove*, *Stanhope*, *Stanholme*, *Stancourt*, *Stanhill* and *Stanthorpe*, all Billmeir ships. There were other ships also, not owned by Billmeir, such as the *Dover Abbey* and *Farnham* with similar claims and the *Surreybrook* with claims for desertions at Barcelona totalling £12 18s 5d. Barcelona was one of the major collecting points for volunteers to the International Brigade, who fought for the Republican cause. Stowaways were a regular occurrence, but one incident at the end of the Spanish Civil War was on a different scale. In March 1939 Archibald Dickson was the master of the 1,383 ton *Stanbrook* with a crew of nineteen and arrived in Alicante, one of the last Nationalist ports, to pick up a cargo. However he had arrived just as thousands of refugees, estimated at 20,000 or more, turned up at the quay desperate to escape. Carrying any cargo was abandoned and records put the total number of refugees carried on board the *Stanbrook* at 2,638 and ten minutes after leaving for the Algerian coast Alicante was heavily bombed. The refugees were safely landed at Oran but the *Stanbrook* was torpedoed in November the same year with the loss of all hands.[34] Much of the claim by then was covered by war risks but the Club also paid out £750.

At the Annual General Meeting in June 1938 a proposal was made that the rules should be changed to 'disallow claims in respect of capture, seizure or consequences of any attempt there at arising from any breach or attempted breach of blockade'. This was deferred to a sub committee consisting of Alfred Stocken and the Chairman, Abbie Anderson. A change to rule 10 regarding liabilities 'whether there be a declaration of war or not' eventually came into force in 1939, too late for the Spanish Civil War which ended in April. On 20th June the Finance Committee of Classes 4 and 5 approved the largest set of claims that had ever

[29] Paul Heaton, *Spanish Civil War Blockade Runners*, (Heaton Publishing, 2006), p. 54
[30] *The Times* 24th December 1963 Obituary
[31] *Lloyd's Register*

[32] Heaton, *Spanish Civil War*, pp. 54-55
[33] P M Heaton, *Jack Billmeir, Merchant Shipowner*, (Newport: Starling Press, 1989), p. 33
[34] *Western Mail* 8th April 2009

been presented to them. The amount involved was in excess of £8,300 with recovery of £3,880. The largest claim for £1,377 was for the *Farnham* which had been bombed.[35]

In 1938 the Coasting Vessel War Risk Association came back into being at the request of the Board of Trade and later the Ministry of War Transport. According to Crowe:

> *An enormous Ministry grew up almost overnight and the result was the most elaborate contracts and method of valuation of ships. Stocken recalled that when the same situation arose in 1917 the contract between the Ministry and the Club was hand written on a single sheet of paper.*[36]

The increase in tonnage and the new direction for Steamship was recognised in 1939 when Sydney Crowe was invited to join Stocken and Plincke as a partner. Shortly afterwards two new companies were set up. The management of the Clubs was to be handled by Alfred Stocken (Managers) Ltd and the brokerage business previously in the name of Steamship Mutual Underwriting Association 'should be carried on by John Plincke & co (Brokerage) and the profits of the same to be payable to the Directors thereof as hitherto'.[37] Crowe and Plincke were directors and shareholders in both firms.

The partners of Alfred Stocken and Company were John Frederick Plincke, Sydney Robert Crowe, Alfred Stephen John Stocken and Edith Joan Lane 'to carry on, develop and turn to account the business of Managers of Mutual Insurance Associations' at 49 Leadenhall Street.[38] Edith Lane is a mystery as no trace has been found of her to suggest what her role was in the new organisation. The share capital was £2,500 divided into £1 shares. John Plincke and Sydney Crowe, described as insurance brokers, held one share each. Sydney Crowe's own recollection was that:

> *When Crowe became a Partner in 1939, Stocken decided to change the partnership to a limited liability company – Alfred Stocken & Co. (Managers) Ltd. saying, fairly enough, that as the impecunious Crowe had saddled the Club with ocean liners (which he considered profitable but dangerous) he and Plincke must avoid having to pay all the partnership liabilities* [39]

Farnham (ex *Marsal*) owned by
H Harrison Shipping Ltd

Stanthorpe, 4,525 grt (ex.*Kambole, Malvern Range*)
owned by Jack Billmeir 1937–38

On the outbreak of another world war the Club had now firmly moved into a new era and had shown itself to be an organisation that was not afraid to reinvent itself as circumstances changed.

War Years

In 1939 the Board of Trade asked the Association to resume cover for war risks and had indicated that it would reinsure cover to the extent of 80 per cent of agreed values on the lines of the legislation laid down in the War Risk Insurance Act 1939. War risks had previously been in operation during the Spanish Civil War between 1936 and April 1939. The policies would follow closely those of other War Risk Clubs and only ships registered under the British flag and with a master of British nationality, born of British parents could be accepted. In addition, Admiralty orders and instructions had to be strictly complied with as well as any special requirements of the Managers and/or the Committee of the Association.[40] Jim Howard-Smith was recruited as a book keeper. He was aged just 19 and childhood polio had prevented him from joining the armed forces.

> I joined SSM on 1st August 1939, being engaged by John Plincke as the book keeper for, I think, £120 pa. At that time the books were being kept by Joseph Ames, father of Geoffrey and Oswald Ames, on a part-time basis and were, of course, written up by hand. Staff consisted of J F Plincke and S R Crowe, partners in Alfred Stocken and Co, E R Howes, Miss Green in the policy department, two typists, a filing clerk and an office boy. We were all housed in a small office suite of 6 rooms in 49 Leadenhall Street.
>
> Most of the business at that time was sailing barges and ketches in the Sailing Ship Mutual Insurance Association and a few coasters and half a dozen deep sea vessels in Steamship Mutual Underwriting Assn. Ltd. We also ran a club for Hull and Machinery risks, the Coastal Vessels Mutual Marine Ins Assn, mainly for Thames Sailing barges which operated within certain specified limits based on Port of London Authority jurisdiction but we also accepted some of the ketches in the Bristol Channel area. All were reinsured by Lloyd's through a contract negotiated by Lyon Lohr & Sly.
>
> Some other hulls and extraneous insurances were accepted when we acted as brokers (John Plincke & Co, Brokerage Ltd) using Lloyds brokers such as Glanville Enthoven & Co & others, with whom we shared the usual 5% brokerage. [41]

By July 1940 there was concern that some members still did not understand what cover was available. As a result an explanatory letter was sent to the members of the Sailing Ship, Steamship and Coasting Vessel Clubs explaining that the best method of obtaining complete marine and war cover was by entry in Class 4 of the P&I Club and in

[35] Sailing Ship Minutes June 1938
[36] Crowe, SSM Club History Notes
[37] Sailing Ship Minutes 1939

[38] A S Stocken (Managers) Ltd Articles of Association
[39] Crowe, SSM Club History Notes
[40] Hooper, Steamship History (draft), p. 72
[41] Jim Howard-Smith, Notes on SSM History, undated c.1983

John Plincke c. 1930s

the War Risk Club. The War Risk Club covered the war risks that were excluded by the P&I Club. However, an owner with an incomplete P&I Club entry, or only a war risk insurance at Lloyd's on Institute War Clauses, would have gaps in his cover.[42] The War Risks were to cause much administration work.

> *We had to issue policies every 91 days, based on a complicated hull value which had to be approved by the Ministry of Transport in each case. Every risk accepted had to be entered by hand in a big Risk book, which detailed the tonnage (or value) and period of the risk, plus the premiums charged. So far as P&I was concerned we debited the instalments quarterly at 1s per grt and made the final call 6 months later, if required. Entrance fees were charged at 1 guinea per 100 tons, minimum 2 guineas & this was the management fee.*[43]

With the advent of war it is apparent that some vessels entered with Steamship Mutual were now no longer restricting themselves to the British coastal trade or the continental trade. On the 4th December 1939 the Managers wrote to the Falklands Islands Co Ltd, E Geraci, McCowen & Gross Ltd, Minster Steamship Co Ltd, Stanhope Steamship Co Ltd and C Strubin & Co Ltd telling them that as a result of the United States Neutrality Act the US Customs were withholding clearance of vessels until affidavits had been filed by the shippers of all cargo consigned to any State which at that time might be at war. This applied not only to cargoes shipped in the United States but also to cargoes in transit from other countries.

Inevitably, with an office based in the City of London and not far from the docks, disruption occurred. In August 1941 the Managers sent the members the Financial Statement/Calls Sheet for the previous year with an apology for a delay due to some disorganisation caused by damage to their offices and the need to evacuate some of the books to the suburbs for greater safety. It was issued in a more abbreviated form than usual to comply with the Government's desire to save paper.[44]

I never saw Alfred Stocken. He had retreated to Newbury Berks for the duration but his house at Richmond became our refuge from the bombing when the air war hotted up & Sydney Crowe spent a lot of his time there with Miss Green the typist, while Howes and I carried on in London with the others. We were joined by Thomas Stocken, Alfred's brother, at this time who was left in charge of the Richmond House & began to take a part in handling a few of the barge claims. We used to have annual condition surveys of most of the Thames barges & these were mainly performed by Horace Shrubsall & his son, H P Shrubsall, barge builder at Gravesend.

The war was a nuisance as we had to collect up all the books, certificates & cash box & other valuables every night & wheel them down to the strong room in the basement. On arrival in the morning we occasionally found all the windows blown in and soot all over the place (we had coal fires then as the only source of heat) but the biggest bang took place when one end of the building was hit and demolished Stocken & Co's office [the solicitors], leaving only the fireplace hanging on the wall. They lost most of their papers which gave them an excellent excuse for delay in dealing with our cases. Cyril Stocken headed the Admiralty department [of Stocken & Co solicitors] assisted by his chief Clerk, Dover and by W Ayres.[45]

Committee meetings were less frequent but the Club continued to grow and 'the assistance of Members in gaining additional tonnage for the Association and making its benefits more widely known was warmly welcomed'. At the close of 1940/41 the Steamship and Sailing Ship combined entered tonnage was 211,889.[46]

One claim that rumbled on through the war was the *Stanwood* owned by Jack Billmeir. While on passage to the River Plate with a cargo of coal it was sunk after a fire in Falmouth harbour. In December 1941 the Managers reported on the salvage contract for the removal of ship and cargo. A procedure had been agreed with reinsurers and owners, which included the acquisition of the underwriters' subrogation rights in which shipowners were participating to the extent of £200. Rather surprisingly the minutes note that 'Mr Crowe added that the Shipowners had sold him personally 50 per cent of this interest for £100'.[47] Attempts were made on many occasions to salvage the wreck but this was not successful until 1950 and the Committee were told that the wreck of the *Stanwood* had

---

[42] Hooper, Steamship History (draft), p. 88
[43] Howard-Smith, Notes on SSM History
[44] Hooper, Steamship History (draft), pp. 75-77

[45] Howard-Smith, Notes on SSM History
[46] Hooper, Steamship History (draft), pp. 74-79
[47] Hooper, Steamship History (draft), p. 74

finally been dispersed and the Harbour Authorities had issued a certificate confirming this. Throughout the war Billmeir's ships continued to be mentioned in claims.

In May 1942 at a Committee meeting the Chairman, Abbie Anderson, read a letter he had received from 'Mr S R Crowe explaining that he had been called up for service in the Navy and apologising for his absence from the meeting'. The Managers were instructed to write to him on behalf of the Chairman and Committee thanking him and wishing him the very best of luck but also 'expressing the hope that he would soon be able to resume his duties as a Manager of the Association'.[48] However, Crowe was not to totally leave the Club behind. He had joined the Royal Navy as a rating and:

> After Sydney Crowe joined the Navy he was given special leave to come back to London to negotiate with the Admiralty certain Club claims involving naval interests. One of the Club secretaries, who had been present during the subsequent meeting, told me that it was a unique sight to see the two senior naval officers negotiating with Sydney in his 'bellbottoms'.[49]

Sydney was made an officer a short time afterwards and spent his war years in a minesweeper.

Houseflag of Stanhope Steamship Co Ltd (Billmeir)

Provident, Brixham trawler insured with Sailing Ship, still operating out of Brixham.

[48] Sailing Ship Minutes 5th May 1942
[49] Howard Morgan, SSM History draft, July 1995

Chapter 3

POST WW2 INTERNATIONALISATION

During the 15 years from the end of the Second World War to the start of the 1960s, Steamship transforms itself from a small regional English mutual to the Club in the London Group with the most international Committee.

Sydney Crowe was demobilised very speedily after the war and his 'early release was obtained in order to liberate John Plincke and to take part in a salvage attempt on the *Stanwood* which was sunk in Carrick Roads, Falmouth & formed the biggest claim on the Club at that time'.[1] So in December 1945 the minutes record the return of Sydney Crowe to 49 Leadenhall Street.[2] Just nine months after his return came the death of Alfred Stocken, who had been ill for some time. With John Plincke also running his brokerage firm this left Sydney as the only full time partner and as he looked at the shipping industry, in Crowe's words 'it was clear that the complexion of the business must change'.[3] Hull insurance of coasters was in decline with so many lost during the war and the days of the sailing barge were numbered, the last barge being built in 1921. However, the war had not been all bad news for some shipowners.

> A large number of the coasting craft and sailing barges were requisitioned on a bare boat basis by the Ministry as mine watching barges and to carry barrage balloons. As the crews were rarely sailormen and requests for docking and painting were ignored, virtually all the wooden craft were riddled with worm or beyond repair at the end of the war. As the days of small coasting craft were drawing to a close before the war, owners thankfully received adequate (some say more than adequate) compensation. One sailing barge owner who was not so fortunate as to lose his craft during the war told one of the Club Managers 'If I owed you a grudge I'd give you my barges'.[4]

Before the war the opportunity for the Club to expand into insuring ocean going vessels was not easy. Pre-war British shipowners were very loyal to their existing Clubs and many of them were Committee members of their Clubs. Crowe, however, saw that matters were now different. 'Deep sea vessels had changed ownership and the new owners did not have the long standing attachments to their Clubs that pre-war owners had.'[5] The changes in the shipping world were profound and Britain now no longer had the largest merchant fleet. 'The only countries whose fleets expanded substantially during the war were the United States and the British Dominions. The dominions principally concerned were Australia, Canada and India.'[6] War torn European countries began to rebuild their fleets. For instance Italy had only 382,000 tons of shipping remaining, which was just 11 per cent of the pre-war total, but by December 1949 the Italians were almost back to their pre-war strength.[7] Additionally, India and Pakistan gained their independence and began the task of acquiring a deep sea fleet.

Indian Entries

The first Indian owned ship, *Bharat Mata*, was entered in the Club in 1945. Within a few years further Indian shipowners joined as well as owners from Pakistan, Brazil, Germany and Italy. Sydney Crowe built up good connections with brokers and other people well connected in the shipping world. He recalled the Indian entry and others:

> *The first such owner entered his ships in the Club and most of the other new Indian owners entered their ships. London insurance brokers started developing their American connections and US flag vessels were entered. The Club was the first to enter the German Market and many ships of that flag were entered when Germany owned ships in her own right again. In 1949 a contract was made with a leading Italian insurance company to enter Italian ships for Protection and Indemnity risks so they could provide a complete cover.[8]*

It looks simple but behind his words lay much hard work, the development of business connections, constant travel in post-war Europe and India and sometimes, luck.

> *A gentleman in Bombay named J B Boda had started to write frequent letters to one of the well established London broking firms. These early letters did not offer*

J B Boda, founder of Crowe Boda

[1] Howard-Smith, Notes on SSM History
[2] Sailing Ship Minutes 18th December 1945
[3] Crowe, SSM Club History notes
[4] Crowe, SSM Club History notes
[5] Crowe, SSM Club History notes; Athlone Press

[6] S G Sturmey, *British Shipping and World Competition* (London, 1962)
[7] *Fairplay* January 1950
[8] Crowe, SSM Club History notes

any business but raised many technical insurance queries – so much so that in the London broker's office the letters were frequently answered by trainees who were studying for their Chartered Insurance Institute examinations. To the London brokers the letters had no particular significance. Then, one day, Boda arrived in London, made his way to the brokers' offices, and placed business totalling about £1 million. The news quickly spread in the market and on Boda's second visit to London some months later three or four brokers sent cars to meet him at Heathrow. However, the important point is that the London brokers principally involved brought Boda to the Steamship Mutual offices. He was appointed general agent in India and soon produced for Steamship Mutual a major part of the developing Indian flag tonnage. The relationship with Jagu Boda was extremely important. It was obvious that he was much respected in the Indian shipping community.[9]

The broker in question was Mr Graham Cory of Muir Beddall & Co who introduced Mr Boda to Steamship.

Mr J B Boda had a very close personal relationship with the Management of Bharat Lines Limited who purchased their first vessel called Bharat Mata *and entered the same with Steamship Mutual on 23rd October 1945 as a first entry from India. Subsequently India Steamship Co., Kolkata (1946) decided to enter their vessels with Steamship Mutual and this was followed by Great Eastern Shipping Co. Ltd.*[10]

One new shipowner was Captain J C Anand of Bombay who had purchased two ageing Liberty ships. These did not look promising from an underwriting viewpoint due to their age. However, Boda persuaded Steamship that they were well maintained and that Anand would be a good shipowner. Indeed his Club record became exemplary and he eventually became Chief Executive of the India Steamship Company. He is remembered as a very straightforward, but hard talking man.[11]

German Entries

One important contact for Sydney Crowe in his mission to grow the Club's tonnage was Norman Leighton. Stelp and Leighton had first set up as steamship owners and at least one of their vessels was insured with Steamship. At some stage they moved out of shipowning and became agents and in the immediate post-war period Norman Leighton was to be a true supporter of Steamship. With his assistance introductions were made to German shipowners in Hamburg and Bremen.

A few first enquiries for P&I cover for German shipowners came from London ships agents and from the Club Correspondents at Hamburg and Bremen. Before the war almost all German shipowners were entered in the Skuld P&I Club of Oslo. After the war the first reaction of the Skuld Club was to refuse to cover any German vessels. While refusing cover for German vessels Skuld did still need claims handling facilities at German ports in connection with non-German ships. Skuld was therefore in contact with the Hamburg and Bremen Club correspondents, and occasionally in

John Niemann, grandson of the founder
of D G Neptun and Committee member
of Steamship from 1956

Minerva, 3,483 grt, built in 1939 owned by Dampfschifffahrts
Gesellschaft "Neptun", Bremen

*contact with a German shipowner, in connection with claims. In all these contacts
the Skuld personnel refused to speak German – despite the fact that the Skuld
staff were fluent in the German language and, indeed, had conducted all pre-war
German business in German. Now, however, Skuld insisted upon all discussion and
correspondence with the Germans being conducted in English.*[12]

Surviving correspondence between J & K Brons, brokers in Bremen and Skuld tells a
subtly different story. In 1948 German shipowners began to seek P&I insurance cover
and contacted Skuld. Skuld's Committee decided the time was not right but the details
of the vessels were requested from the German owners. In June 1948 the formal reply
from Skuld was that the 'Committee has however decided that we still must await the
formal solution of war before resuming activities in your country'. Meanwhile Brons was
recommending three British Clubs, the UK Club, Newcastle P&I and West of England to
their clients. By 22nd March 1949 Skuld had contacted the Norwegian 'department of
foreign affairs' who said they were 'not allowed to take over P&I insurance on German
vessels' although Skuld believed the situation would be resolved shortly. Crowe, with
assistance from Leighton, visited the firms and successfully entered five vessels belonging
to the DG Neptun Line of Bremen in the teeth of a competing bid from the UK Club for the
same vessels.[13] These were *Minerva*, *Zeus*, *Olbers*, *Latona* and *Theseus* and they were all
entered with Steamship from noon on 20th August 1949.[14] The British clubs were active

---

[9] Morgan, SSM History draft
[10] Email Mr Dhanki to H Doe, 8th April 2009
[11] Anthony Crowe interview, 14th January 2009
[12] Morgan, SSM History draft

[13] DG Neptun; Letter UK Club to Brons 31st Jan 1949
[14] Steamship Policy Document 25th Aug 1949; H Juniel
Fax 12th July 1999

and successful in the German market. The United Kingdom Club obtained the Hamburg-Amerika Line, Norddeutscher Lloyd and a few other large fleets, while the West of England and Steamship Mutual concentrated on the middle of the range shipowners and Sunderland had mainly smaller owners.

The various difficulties in Norway were eventually resolved in September 1950 and finally through its Danish office, Skuld formally offered the provision of cover to German vessels in a letter in both German and English. For some shipowners this was too late and in December 1951 Skuld was writing direct to German shipowners such as DG Neptun in an attempt to win back their business by showing that, since September 1950, 41 German ships of 40,623 tons were now entered.[15] The British Clubs, in particular Steamship, gained considerably from the situation.

> *The Germans were receiving international financial aid to facilitate the rebuilding of their merchant marine fleet and many new ships were being completed throughout each year. In the early 1950s for the Club Manager it was often just a case of visiting the shipowner at the right time i.e. shortly before a new ship was due to come into service. The freight market was good and everyone so occupied that the shipowner would sometimes sign a blank Club entry form, leaving the Club representative to fill in the details.[16]*

Within a few years Steamship Mutual had about 1 million grt of German shipping.[17] In June 1949 the Lloyd Brasileiro fleet of eighteen ships purchased from the US Maritime Commission were entered and the minutes noted that 'Satisfactory business continued to come through the leading Lloyd's brokers'. The other highly successful introduction was to the Italian market and one company in particular was to provide Steamship Mutual with very significant business.

Italian Entries

Crowe obtained introductions through Robert Bradford and Company to Ernesto and Ugo Fassio, two brothers based in Genoa who had various interests including an insurance society, Levante, that provided hull insurance.[18] Ernesto was the controlling shareholder but due to his other business interests, which included a newspaper and a shipping line, he left the active management of the insurance company to his younger brother.

> *Ugo Fassio had devoted his whole time and attention to Levante and had succeeded in building it up into a major Italian company. Ugo knew personally every important Italian shipowner. Ugo quickly recognised the importance of P&I cover for Italian shipowners and the desirability of Levante being in a position to offer this additional cover. An agreement was made under which Levante became general agents in Italy for Steamship Mutual. Levante estimated that it would produce 1 million grt of Italian P&I business for Steamship Mutual within one year. It was difficult for the London contingent to believe that this was possible but in the event, the estimate proved to be no exaggeration. Some Italian shipowners covered P&I for the first time but many*

were persuaded to transfer from other Clubs – particularly the United Kingdom Club which had a significant number of Italian Members. The United Kingdom Club's senior manager made his displeasure known at the loss of the tonnage but Steamship Mutual was under no obligation to contact him because Steamship Mutual had not at that time been admitted to the London Group of Clubs and did not have to support expiring terms and rates. In practice rating was not an important factor in the transfers and the first three years of the Italian business were remarkably profitable.[19]

Liberty Ships

It was the American surplus of shipping that was indirectly responsible for Steamship's rapid expansion into international shipping. By 1945 the US had the largest merchant marine in the world, but much of this was now surplus with an estimated 14 million grt in the reserve fleet.[20] Foreign fleets took 1,100 ships including many Liberty ships at bargain prices. Many found their way into British, Russian, Dutch, Norwegian and notably, Greek merchant fleets. By the early 1960s it is estimated that the Liberty ship constituted about 40 per cent of the world tramp fleet.[21] These ships, of which over 2,700 were built, were based on a design adapted from a British Sunderland type coal burning tramp. The Americans with their considerable manufacturing skill and organisation produced them in factory line conditions, beating all records for speed of building.[22] Four US shipyards produced the T2 tanker, also built to a standard design and over 200 of these were sold to foreign buyers.[23]

Rialto, 7,153 grt Liberty ship owned by
Cia Armatoriale Italiana, Venice

Ambronia, 10,397 grt T2 tanker Amerocean
Steamship Co Inc, Genoa

[15] DG Neptun; Skuld to Brons 22 March 1949; J & K Brons to DG Neptun 18 July 1950; Skuld to DG Neptun 7th September 1950, 5th December 1951, 10th March 1952

[16] Morgan, SSM History draft

[17] Morgan, SSM History draft

[18] Howard-Smith, Notes on SSM History

[19] Morgan, SSM History draft

[20] *Lloyd's Register of Shipping Annual Report* 1949/50

[21] Robert Gardiner, (ed), *The Shipping Revolution: The Modern Merchant Ship*, (Bath: Conway Maritime Press, 1992), p.17

[22] Gardiner, *The Shipping Revolution*, pp. 16-17

[23] http://www.mariners-l.co.uk/T2.html

The availability of the Liberty ships and T2 tankers alone was not the reason for the rapid expansion of P&I insurance. One of the requirements of the mortgages, such as those provided by the US Department of Commerce, was the obligation to obtain P&I insurance in order that the mortgagee could be fully covered in the event of the loss of the vessel.[24] Shipowners who had never previously considered such types of insurance were now targeted by the Clubs. While many shipowners continued their cover even when this stipulation was no longer in force, this was not always the case. In 1956 two Italian owners told the Club they no longer wished to continue to insure for P&I as they no longer had a mortgage need.[25] But one additional factor that encouraged Italian shipowners was the tragic explosion in the port of Naples of the Italian T2 tanker *Montallegro* in March 1951. There had been heavy loss of life and damage to property. The hull insurance was with the Levante Insurance Company and the P&I with Steamship Mutual. As Lanfranco Spechel, who was then with the Levante, recalls:

> Italian owners then realised that P&I was important but did not know what Protection & Indemnity meant as there was not a 'proper' insurance policy that they were familiar with but just a piece of paper showing the date of attachment, the expiry date which was the 20th of February and a reference to 'the book of Rules'. It seems that nobody in Italy was able to explain what was being covered.
>
> This was the reason why the Levante decided to send somebody to London for over 3 years. On my return to Genoa in 1956 I became known as the P&I expert with a non-Italian name and speaking Italian with an English accent. I remember an owner in Genoa phoning the Levante asking who was the foreigner they had sent to see him.[26]

American Business

Since 1942 the Club had covered small American and Canadian craft (fishing boats, tugs, barges and coasters) on a fixed premium basis.[27]

> Lloyd's brokers brought in 'slips' requesting quotations to cover the crew risk on New England fishing vessels. This risk would normally be covered in the US domestic market but the US producing brokers were happy to allow their London counterparts to explore alternatives. Lloyd's would not take the primary risk because of involvement in detailed claims handling. The business was producing only small premium income e.g. perhaps US $100 per crewmember per annum, fixed premium, but the Club cover could be restricted to a low limit. As long as the Club was prepared to cover the primary risk (and attend to the claims handling) Lloyd's was happy to quote for the excess. It seemed desirable for the Club to underwrite this business on a modest scale because the creation of a new market would bring frequent visits from influential Lloyd's brokers who might well introduce ocean going mutual business.[28]

People and Club Changes

This rate of increased business required an expansion of staff from its 1945 establishment of just eight people and there were organisational changes also.[29] By 1947 the Committee was being asked to consider the desirability of separating Steamship Mutual Underwriting Association Limited, covering steamers and motor vessels over 200 tons gross, from Sailing Ship Mutual Insurance Association Limited, covering sailing and motor barges and similar small craft under 200 tons. The two Clubs began operating separately with effect from 20th February 1947. The estimated reserve for unreported claims at the time of the split was recorded as £9,148 of which £7,198 was allocated to Steamship Mutual. With regard to American fixed premium business, a further £2,000 for unreported claims was retained by Sailing Ship Mutual, with the final adjustment to be made when the policies had run off and all claims and returns had been settled.[30]

Abbie Anderson naturally continued as Chairman of both and at the age of 72 he showed no sign of slowing down or retiring. At the Annual General Meeting in September 1949 a special resolution was unanimously carried that 'No person shall be required to retire from or vacate his office as a member of the Committee for a period of three years from this date by reason of his having attained the age of seventy or any other age'. If he had orchestrated this it did not in the end have much implication for him as his death was announced six months later. He had been active right up to the Committee meeting a few months before. Mr E A Gill was elected Chairman for the meeting and he spoke of Mr Anderson with affection and said that many members of the Association had attended his funeral. However, he added, in his view in future it would be a good thing if the Chair changed hands annually. The Committee, not surprisingly, unanimously agreed.[31]

Abbie Anderson

Abbie was born on the 16th March 1877. He lived and worked at Whitstable throughout his life and had been a member of the Association since the absorption of the Whitstable Club in 1911. His father, Captain Absalom Anderson, was a Master Mariner in the foreign trade. On his death at a comparatively early age, Abbie took over the family's coal and shipping interests. In company with his brother-in-law Alfred Gann, who was also a Committee member and Charles Perkins they set up a company known as Anderson, Rigden and Perkins. As well as his involvement with the Steam and Sailing Ship Clubs Abbie also sat on various committees within the Chamber of Shipping. He played a leading part in the Government sponsored scheme to develop a number of small ports including Rye

[24] G. Harlaftis, *Greek Shipowners and Greece, 1945–1975*, (London; Athlone Press, 1993), pp. 50-51; Lanfranco Spechel Notes 2008

[25] Steamship Minutes February 1956

[26] L Spechel Notes

[27] Steamship Minutes, add. typed note 25th September 1953, p. 120

[28] Morgan, SSM History draft

[29] Crowe, SSM History notes

[30] Sailing Ship Minutes, February 1947

[31] Sailing Ship Minutes, May 1950

Abbie Anderson, long serving chairman,
pictured outside Anderson, Rigden and Perkins,
shipbuilders of Whitstable, Kent

and was an active member of many other committees.[32] In Sailing Ship Mutual he had been a Committee member since 28th January 1913 and had served for the first time as Chairman of Classes 1, 2 and 6 on 2nd April 1919. He had been the Chairman of these Classes, as well as Classes 4 and 5, and Chairman of Steamship from 1925 until his death.

Steamship Mutual in 1951

The list of ships entered in the Club for 1951 shows the major change in the membership. It now stood at 1,152,620 tons, the million benchmark having been reached on 28th February 1950 at Abbie Anderson's last meeting. It is perhaps appropriate that it was also at this meeting that Norman Leighton was attending as a Committee member. He was 'warmly welcomed' and with good reason as it was his contacts that had helped to bring so much business to the Club. The chart shows how the country share changed.

By 1951 the majority of the vessels entered which were owned in the UK were of small tonnage. There were 129 UK registered ships, 96 of which were under 500 tons. The largest vessel was the *Stanford*, entered at 5,968 tons, owned by Jack Billmeir and now the only ship in his fleet that he had with the Club. The rest of Billmeir's ships were now insured with the UK Club of which he was a Director. The 82 Italian ships had a total tonnage of 573,031 and made up half of the Club. The smallest craft insured was the 80 ton

Mainmoor owned by the Air Ministry and the oldest vessel on the books was the 1877 built 117 ton *Lizzie & Annie* of Hull owned by the B W Steamship, Tug & Lighter Co Ltd.

In world tonnage terms, Steamship was just beginning as it insured only 1 per cent of world ships. However, within that it insured 20 per cent of the Italian fleet, 12 per cent of the German fleet, 7 per cent of the Brazilian fleet and 9 per cent of the Commonwealth fleet (India and Pakistan were not at the time reported separately).[33]

The Managers

There was a minor change to the name of the Managers which became just Alfred Stocken & Company Ltd in 1951. The bigger change was less obvious to outsiders. From just two shares held by Crowe and Plincke in 1941, by December 1954 the shares issue had changed to 62 designated preference shares, 1,438 ordinary shares and 1,000 special shares.[34] The Managers were looking to expand their organisation and Crowe had recruited new staff members; Howard Morgan first appeared in the minutes in 1953 and Alan Tolhurst arrived in 1954.

Chart 2: Steamship entered tonnage by country of registration 1950 and 1953, in thousands (from ships entered and *Lloyd's Register*)

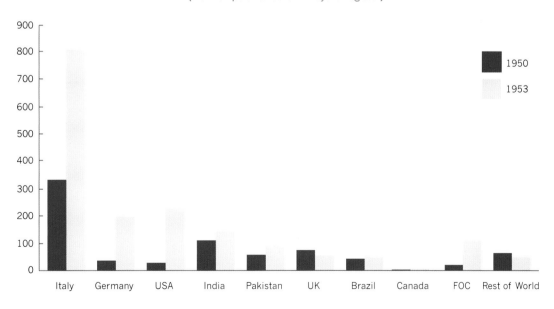

[32] R K Anderson to D Hooper, 10th October 1999; *Whitstable Times and Tankerton Press*, obituary 1950

[33] *Lloyd's Register* Annual Report 1952
[34] A Stocken & Co Annual Return 1954

The Office in 1954

As mentioned earlier, Lanfranco Spechel came at the request of the Genoese based Levante company 'to learn as much as possible about P&I'.[35] Levante had become the Italian agents for Steamship Mutual in June 1952.[36] When Lanfranco arrived in March 1953 he found that :

> *Life in London was quite different to what I was used to in Italy. The room booked for me in Gloucester Road was very large but very dim with only one bed, one chest of drawers, a cupboard, a table and a chair. It was also quite cold. On my arrival there, after a journey of 36 hours by train from Rome with only a few sandwiches in my bag, I was looking forward to a big breakfast but was given only a herring with toast and an undrinkable coffee. My landlady told me that some food, like butter, milk and meat was rationed and that I should apply to the Home Office for my ration card. Because the heat was produced mainly by coal, fog could be very bad specially during the night and traffic slow, making it impossible to arrive anywhere on time.*

> *Steamship Mutual's office was not far away from the docks and from Lloyd's. It was in an old building and located on two separate floors (the second and the fourth I recall). The whole staff at that time was 17 people to become 18 on my arrival. The lift was water driven and the lift 'boy' was an elderly man in a bright red uniform wearing thick leather gloves to pull on the ropes. It was amazing to me that he would stop the lift at exactly the same level as the floor.[37]*

Peter and Tony Crowe can remember accompanying their father to the office. It was a dark building with glass panels above wooden partitions, coal fires, mats, rugs and domestic lighting. Tony recalls many cased yard models of ships. As an office junior Dave Gurton had to ensure the fires were supplied with coal, but he can also recall tea and toast by the fire in the afternoon. Doreen McDonnell, a typist, recalls sitting shivering as she took dictation from Sydney Crowe whose large frame was sitting behind his desk and between her and the fire.[38]

Carl Fisser, general cargo vessel, owned by Fisser Schiffahrt GmbH in Nov. 1962 at quayside in Kings Dock, Swansea

Bharat Kumar, 1,645 grt owned by Bharat Line Ltd, Bombay

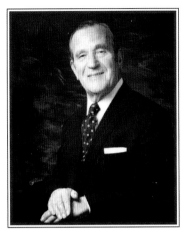

Boardroom portrait of Sydney Crowe

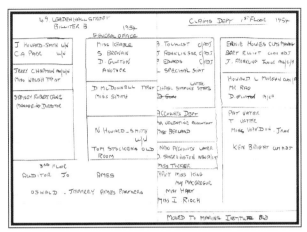

Floor plan of 49 Leadenhall Street in the 1950s

On the fourth floor there were the offices of the Senior Partner and Chairman, Alfred Stocken, the Executive Officer Sydney Crowe and the underwriters Jim Howard-Smith and Clifford Parr.

> *I was close to Mr J Howard-Smith and had a table not much larger than a bedside table fully taken by the Rules, a dictionary,* Templeman on Marine Insurance, *and a note book. The most sought-after person was Miss Keeble who knew everything about the office and where to find what everybody else had given up for lost. She did not look at all young, but was still there many years after I had gone.*

> *The claims department on the second floor was headed by Mr Howes and Mr H Morgan and Mr A Tolhurst who had joined Steamship Mutual a few days before my arrival was also in that department (we became great friends and I was his best man when he later married Margaret).*[39]

Mr Howes, the person taken on as the travelling 'salesman' for the Club, was still there:

> *Mr Howes' main activity was handling claims related to barges trading regularly between north and south of England. He was alleging that he had to keep in touch every day at 11.30 a.m., returning at 3.00 p.m.*

> *Mr Crowe was not at all happy about this situation and one day he told Mr. Howes to stop going out and instead to have his coffee in the office, the same as every body*

[35] L Spechel Notes
[36] Steamship Minutes June 1952
[37] L Spechel Notes
[38] Anthony Crowe January 2009, Peter Crowe letter 25th November 2009, Dave Gurton, Doreen McDonnell interview December 2008
[39] L Spechel Notes

else. Having said this the following morning he came to the claims department and bumped into Mr. Howes, who was about to leave the office, and asked where he was going – "to meet my barge owners friends, Sir" was his reply: as a result Mr. Howes was downgraded and Mr H. Morgan became the Head of the Department. Mr. Howes kept meeting his barge owners down at the local.

It is fair to say that barge insurance was important to the Club at the time but was quickly being overtaken by Indian, American white water fixed premium business and a fast growing Italian business.[40]

Barge owners were not men to be easily dismissed and one famous incident told many times over was the moment when Sammy Single, a barge owner, came to the office to remonstrate with Jim Howard-Smith who had refused a claim. Jim was at that time the image of the classic London city gentleman. His daughter recalls his dark suit, bowler hat, tightly rolled umbrella and each morning he cut a fresh flower from his garden for his lapel.[41] So the office staff were much amused by the sight of him being poked in the chest with a pipe by the irate barge owner who demanded 'Now look here, Smithy, you pay my claim!'[42]

Even though I handled many hundreds – even thousands – of claims in my time, I still remember discussing a claim for water damage to ten bags of grain carried by a barge, with one of the Shrubsall Brothers. No one told me that he used to be a Committee Member of one of the Clubs.[43]

Claims

In a still rationed Britain there were the inevitable cargo shortage claims. In 1946 the *Edenvale*'s cargo of stockings was inexplicably short (a claim of £278) and the *Chelsea*'s cargo of kerosene was also short, a claim of £215. Generally shortages and pilfering were on the increase and preventative steps needed to be taken, such as assisting the Wexford Steamship Company to redraft their bills of lading. Crowe travelled to Ireland to achieve this.[44] Smuggling was another problem. While on voyage from Dublin to Silloth with a general cargo the *St Fintan* had been rummaged by the Customs at Douglas and had been seized. 'Considerable quantities of cigarettes & stockings had been found & the vessel, being under 250 tons was declared forfeit.' It was released on payment of £2,500 by Messrs Stocken & Co (solicitors) who were able to obtain a refund of £2,300 on proving 'the Shipowners had taken all possible steps to prevent smuggling by the crew and had given every assistance when the contraband was discovered'. There was no prosecution of the crew as all had denied any knowledge.[45] There were also the wartime wrecks to be sorted. The *Atlantic Scout* was wrecked in Boulogne and in September 1947 the Club sought advice from a legal representative in Paris and additionally expert advice from Mr Cyril Miller, senior partner in Millers and Secretary of the British Maritime Law Association.[46]

With more tonnage the list of claims was growing and the increasingly international nature involved more complexity and, for the Managers, more travel. One new recruit who

Saint Fintan owned by T Heiton and Co

il fusto - cask
il faro - light house
i fondali - soundings
firmase - to sign.
la fasciama - outer plate.
le fasce elastiche - elastic belting.
il fondo di cilindro - cylinder head
 "   "   " stantuffo - piston head
la feritoia - vent hole
il fondello - bottom plate
il foro - hole, tunnel

Extract from dictionary belonging to Sally
Howard-Smith (née Moore)

[40] L Spechel Notes
[41] Bridget Wayman conversation
[42] Dave Gurton, 10th December 2008
[43] Hooper, Steamship History (draft), p. 68

[44] Sailing Ship Minutes 3rd December 1946
[45] Steamship Minutes 8th March 1951
[46] Sailing Ship Minutes September 1947;
    Fairplay, March 1950

Indian Merchant, Victory type, owned by India
Steamship Company Ltd, Calcutta

Yarmouth Castle and her sister ship *Evangeline*

was essential for the fast changing Club was Sally Moore, who spoke several languages.
Sally had been to a finishing school in Lausanne and then had been to a secretarial
college and joined Steamship in 1950. Her language skills were of considerable value and
her daughter still has the book into which Sally entered the translations of the various
specialist maritime terms in Italian, French, Spanish and German. Sally later married Jim
Howard-Smith and left the Club when she had her first child, which was the usual practice
for women in the 1950s.[47]

In 1949 the *Indian Pioneer* was involved in a claim arising from the destruction of 640
tons of maize, for which legal proceedings had commenced in New York for $75,000 with
costs and interest at 6 per cent. Eventually Crowe was able to report to the Committee
the result of his investigations. The cause of the damage was not definite but it was
reported to the Committee that it 'probably arose from a latent defect in the shell plating'.
The Club's New York attorneys advised that the unrecovered costs in the event of the
judgement for the shipowners would be about $13,500. 'Consequently Mr Crowe after
completing enquiries in Bombay and Calcutta had met the Indian Ministry concerned
at New Delhi and after discussion had agreed settlement of $22,500 free of cost and
interest. Attorneys in New York and London considered this an excellent settlement in the
circumstances.'[48]

The Committee, which consisted at this time of British shipowners, was keeping a
careful eye on the expansion of entries and, in particular, the rise in claims and there were
questions put to the managers who were asked to keep running records of the claims
of the German, Indian and the new Italian business. Such concern was inevitable from
a group of men who had been familiar with the pre-war Club in which they had personal
knowledge of many Club members and the Committee needed to make adjustments and
learn new ways of scrutinising the business. One fleet was appearing on the claims list
with regularity and in January 1951 an 'Informal Committee meeting' was held to look
at the 'cargo claims experienced by the India Steamship Company's fleet after one and
half years working on liner terms from UK to India'. It was apparent that, although precise
figures were not available, each voyage showed a loss of which a certain proportion could

be regarded as inevitable. It was agreed that the terms of entry of this fleet should be amended either by an increased franchise or by a surcharge for general cargo claims or both. It was eventually decided to increase deductible franchise on cargo claims from £200 to £700. Some claims however were happily resolved. On arrival at Calcutta in July 1949 the cargo of railway material on board the *Indian Merchant*, was found to be 125 tons short. Examination of the tally sheets confirmed a heavy shortage. The progress of the material had been investigated from Wolverhampton to Liverpool and then from Liverpool to Calcutta. Eventually a reward was offered for the discovery of the missing material and in January 1953 the Indian Railways reported that the missing material had been found in their own warehouses. The claim was withdrawn.[49]

In 1952 the outcome of the official enquiry on the *Montallegro* explosion in Italy suggested that the owners were jointly responsible with the repairers and the chemist who signed the gas-free certificate. The total claim was anticipated between £20,000 and £25,000, but in the end the final bill was over £65,000.[50] In 1954 came a potentially very much larger claim from the USA, which was indicative of future liabilities. The ship in question was the 5,000 ton *Yarmouth Castle*, a passenger vessel operating between Miami and the West Indies. One passenger had broken her ankle and, together with 75 other passengers, was claiming food poisoning from chocolate éclairs. One writ had already been issued for $100,000 and further writs were due. The anticipated total bill could potentially be $1 million.[51] While the records do not reveal what happened to this claim, this particular ship later became notorious for the fire that broke out in 1965 with the loss of many passengers and crew. It was not then insured by Steamship Mutual but the resultant enquiry led to many changes in international regimes for safety at sea.

The claims were increasing in size and another problem was strikes. While strikes by seamen were not unusual they were less able to organise themselves as effectively as the men on shore. A Strike Class was proposed in 1956 and at the time it was decided not to go ahead. Another sign of the post-war changes and the increasing move from personal management of all aspects of shipowning was in the debate on crewing. In 1949 the Club was affiliated with the Shipping Federation, an organisation that took a hard line on strikes. Mr Metcalf of Metcalf Motors was already a member of the Council and added that 'while under pre-war conditions he found he could select his crews and get better men by personal contact, war time and post-war conditions of labour probably made membership of the Federation essential'.

[47] Bridget Wayman email 9th May 2009
[48] Steamship Minutes March 1949
[49] Steamship Minutes March 1953

[50] Steamship Minutes 1952
[51] Steamship Minutes 1955; Note: all $ are US dollars

Accidents at Sea

On 29th July 1950 what was described as a

> *...simple, though fitting, ceremony took place on the* Indian Trader *at the position where the* Indian Enterprise *disappeared on 19th June last. All hands not on duty were on the fore deck and two wreaths were cast adrift – one from the owners, the India Steamship Company Limited, Calcutta, and one from the Red Sea Shipping Company (Sudan) Limited. A short silence was observed and the Company's house flag and the ensigns of India, Britain and Pakistan, were flown at half mast.*[52]

The *Indian Enterprise* had exploded and only one crew member survived out of the 74 crewmen. She was carrying 8,530 tons of general cargo and 580 tons of explosives. The Board of Trade wreck report mentioned that the 'ships husband' was Norman Leighton of Stelp and Leighton. The subsequent enquiry was inconclusive and could only point towards the possibility of self ignition of the explosives.[53]

Meanwhile there were claims relating to the rapid expansion of the motor industry with the problems of transporting large numbers of cars unboxed.[54] Shipboard falls were still a regular claim often arising from badly fitted or insecure hatch covers. One man, Jones, was paralysed from the waist down after falling into the hold of the *Eilian Hill* when removing the hatches, some of which had not been replaced from the previous day. A settlement of £10,000, possibly in an annuity, was anticipated. Unfortunately for Jones his writ could not be served as the shipowner had died. The Committee agreed that no advantage should be taken of a 'purely technical defence' and agreed that, subject to the agreement of the owner's executors, that the solicitors Messrs Stocken & Co. should accept service of the writ on behalf of the Club.[55]

The Committee continued to recognise those who saved lives at sea. A seaman had fallen between the ship and the quay when boarding the *Banntrader* at night. His cries for help were heard by the master who, although he could not swim, climbed down the slippery piling and held up the man until further help arrived. The owners wanted to make an award to Captain Mann, who had also ruined his suit, but hesitated in case this would cause the seaman, who was only slightly injured, to make a claim, which he had so far shown no signs of doing. The Committee recognised the 'brave action of Captain Mann and asked the owners on their behalf to make a payment up to £25'.[56] Another payment was made to the P&O Line for expenses incurred in 'laying down oil and in standing by securing boats, crews etc' in the case of the *Allegra*. The payment proposed was £500 which the master would distribute to 'such members of the crew of *Carthage* as had played an active part in the life saving operations'.[57]

London Group of P&I Clubs

This sudden expansion of Steamship into the international market ruffled a few feathers in the world of P&I as described by one of the junior managers at the time. The UK Club in particular made their displeasure known as several of the Italian vessels had previously been insured with them.[58] The UK Club was the largest of the P&I Clubs with over 9 million tons entered at the time and their senior partner was Dawson Miller who was known for his outspoken views.[59] A small skirmish developed to the potential advantage of the Italians. The Managers reported that they had been requested by the Levante society to increase the protection rebates given to Italian vessels for the year 1951/52. When the vessels were first accepted for the year 1950/51 the rebate given for excluded risks was agreed at 30 per cent of the protection calls, that is to say on the same basis as they were formerly accepted by the UK Club. After the latter had lost their entries to Steamship renewal terms for 1951/52 were being offered with a 40 per cent rebate on protection calls and 20 per cent on indemnity calls where vessels were carrying bulk cargoes only. It was agreed that 'as the final cost of a vessel entered in this Association was lower than would be the case under the new rebates offered by the UK Association, the present terms would be continued until greater experience was gained when the position would be fully reviewed'.[60]

The increased competitive strength of Steamship resulted in membership of the London Group of P&I Clubs. Among other things this achieved a greater spread of risk for Steamship, greater lobbying power and recognition of their international status.

> *The increased Club tonnage had brought other serious claims and by the end of 1954 the leading underwriter on the Lloyd's Excess Policy was demanding a 300 per cent increase in premium for the Club year commencing 20th February 1955. It was at this point that it became even more desirable for SSM to obtain admission to the London Group Pool. A previous application, sponsored by Sir John Rutherford of the Sunderland P&I Club, had failed to gain acceptance by a majority of Group Members. By this time, however, the situation had changed. Steamship Mutual had been competing vigorously and Group Clubs had been losing tonnage. In particular, the United Kingdom Club was concerned at the substantial transfer to SSM of Italian ships following the very successful efforts of the Levante company as general agents for SSM in Italy. The outcome of this second application was that the London Group agreed to admit SSM to Membership with effect from 20th February 1955. It appeared to be the general view that it would be better to have Steamship Mutual as a Member adhering to Group underwriting understandings. Happily for SSM the special Lloyd's policy was no longer needed and the 300 per cent proposed premium increase was avoided.[61]*

[52] *Fairplay* 21st September 1950
[53] Board of Trade wreck report for *Indian Enterprise*, 8th January 1951
[54] Steamship Minutes 1952, *Indian Exporter* problems of unboxed cars
[55] Steamship Minutes 1950
[56] Steamship Minutes 15th December 1953
[57] Steamship Minutes 15th October 1958
[58] Anon, 'Steamship History notes', undated
[59] *Fairplay* 21st September 1950; Anon, 'Steamship History notes'
[60] Steamship Minutes, 1953
[61] Morgan, SSM History draft

Finance

The Club Managers were dealing with more sophisticated finances. The days of the small group of sailing shipowners who all knew each other and whose ships stayed firmly in British coastal waters had gone. In 1948 some claims were now handled wholly in American dollars, of the 52 claims reported to the Committee on 7th September 1948, 20 per cent were in dollars and at the time came to a total of $8,050. The Club held both dollars and sterling and in New York bail bonds were needed. The Club's cash situation was changing rapidly and investment strategies had to be considered. At a meeting in 1949, although one member pointed out the 'small but profitable investment available in the Post Office Savings Bank', professional advice was sought and Mr Stephens of Messrs. Gastrell & Co became the Club's stockbroker. His first advice was the purchase of National War Bonds.

By 1950 the managers reported investment of $100,000 in US Treasury bonds. The cash at bank and invested was £162,647 and approximately £40,000 was due. It was agreed that managers should look at the question of investment and 'that a policy should be developed for the next meeting'. By 1956 the Club was tentatively investing in equities and a Committee member, Peter Dorey, was particularly keen on these suggesting that the investment share should be raised from 3 per cent to 10 per cent and that Canadian growth equities should be considered.

The first closure of the Suez Canal came in 1956 when it was nationalised by Nasser who seized control from the British and the French. It was closed to shipping for a year and caused major problems. Up until now the shipping world had seen almost constant growth but shipping now entered a depression and the effect was felt by the Club. In May 1958 the Finance Committee was taking a keen interest in outstanding premiums 'as they felt that given the present slump in shipping there would be an increase in bad debts unless the position was watched very closely'. [62] The next year there was a big debate over the accounts and many question asked of the auditors, Ames & Co, and the Managers. It

Indian Success, 9,458 grt owned by India
Steamship Company Ltd, Calcutta

Jala Dharma, Great Eastern Shipping Co Ltd, Bombay

was eventually agreed that to meet the deficit 'a call would be required under Protection class of 65 per cent and on the Indemnity Class of 25 per cent with double indemnity call for general cargo vessels. This would be equivalent of a seven per cent increase in costs over those for 1956/7'.[63]

Indian Agency

The Club was now having to deal with the challenges of different, and changing, legal and tax regimes in the countries within which its members were based and this threatened expansion in some cases. There had been no insurance either Hull or P&I available in India but now there was an Indian Hull company and the Indian Government's restriction on funds going out of India meant the Indian owners had to insure in India, although reinsurance was 90 per cent in the London market. It was feared that P&I would be next. The proposal by Crowe was to investigate the setting up of an Indian Agency in anticipation of this together with Mr Boda 'our firm and trusted friend'.[64] Although first discussed in 1953 it did not become reality until 1956 when Crowe Boda was established and it had to be managed in a way that reassured the existing Indian members, several of whom were resistant to the initial idea.[65]

The setting up of the agency was a big step and the memories of Abbie Anderson's long rule as Chairman were also still fresh. Mr Metcalf reminded members that, although it was 'a recent custom for the Association that the Chairman held office for one year only', this year he proposed the reappointment of Mr Norman Leighton as Chairman for 1957 as

[62] Steamship Minutes 29th May 1958
[63] Steamship Minutes August 1958
[64] Steamship Minutes 1953, Committee note
[65] Steamship Minutes May 1957 p. 193

he felt that continuity this year was desirable, particularly in view of the 'negotiations that were continuing on the formation of an Indian branch'.[66]

> *Mr Boda initially did the P&I business in the name of J B Boda & Co. Pvt. Limited along with their main insurance and reinsurance broking business. This continued for a number of years and Steamship Mutual, during that period, were seriously thinking to open their Branch in India to transact the P&I business. In spite of Mr. Boda trying his best with various authorities, this was not possible because the Indian Insurance Act did not permit any company to do business on mutual basis i.e. on no loss no profit basis.*
>
> *Having got the independence from Britishers after almost two hundred years, there were also strong feelings to develop more national expertise and, in this process, India became Republic in 1950.*
>
> *Since it was not possible for Steamship Mutual to open a Branch in India and Mr Sydney Crowe also had developed a good rapport and goodwill in the Indian shipping market, Mr Boda thought of separating P&I business by starting a new company jointly with Mr Sydney Crowe and other partners and named it as Crowe Boda & Co. Pvt. Ltd. This company was registered and started operations in 1956. Mr Crowe had no financial interest in the company. However, he and other two partners were named as Directors of Crowe Boda after the necessary permission from the concerned Indian authorities.[67]*

The same year there was also a plan to establish an American branch. The Managers had investigated the possibilities of setting up an American branch as this business was 'subject to 4 per cent Federal Tax and complicated further by the fact that the Club was not an admitted carrier for Federal and the State Workman's Compensation Acts'. This is still an issue in 2009.[68] The possibility of setting up in Rhode Island was considered and steps had been taken to establish one that would, however, remain dormant until further

Esperanza, 4,953 grt owned by Christian Ahrenkiel, Hamburg

details of the costs of such an operation were known.[69] There had been some previous problems in 1953 when a Rhode Island company which was reinsuring business in the US went into liquidation with a debt to the Club of $101,000 with a further of $10,400 for outstanding claims.[70] By 1957 the Club was expecting to receive 50 per cent of the amount involved.[71]

The International Club

Being a truly international Club meant the development of a world wide contact system of correspondents and agents in different ports who were at hand to assist shipping. In 1939 letters had been written to 30 agents inviting them to act as agents for the Club as the letter pointed out 'A number of vessels entered in this Association including Cie France Navigation Fleet frequent your port'. This suggests that the Club was insuring at least one French fleet pre-war although there is no other evidence for this. Then the requirement for agents was for those based in Mediterranean or North European ports but now the Club needed to develop a wider geographical network.[72] An effective and competent agent saved many miles of travel for the Managers, although both Crowe, Morgan and now Alan Tolhurst were constantly on the move.[73] Continental Europe was easier to get to but air travel to the US was still lengthy so there was mention of a 'particularly competent agent in New York, Mr Munroe' acting in several cases. In London the increasing number of staff meant that new premises were needed.[74] By the end of the 1950s the Club was a substantial organisation with investments of over £1 million, reporting to the Committee in January 1959 cash and investments of £1,223,681.[75]

In 1952 the Committee recognised the scale of the international business and Franz Stickan of Neptun Line was co-opted on to the Committee in June. At the Annual General Meeting in October his position was confirmed and Ernesto Fassio, Achille Lauro and Conte Salvatore Tagliavia also became Committee members. By 1958 Mr Sheth, the Managing Director of Great Eastern, was proposed as a member of the Committee, but he would be represented by Mr Robinson, a director of Eggar, Forester & Verner Ltd, their London agents.[76] The use of proxies had originally been rejected by the Committee, but the problems of travel simply made this impossible. In practice this meant that several Committee members never physically attended meetings, but did receive all the papers. In 1960 Steamship truly became the most international of all the British based Clubs when it appointed its first non-British resident as Chairman, Dr Kurt Von Laun of DG Neptun Line of Bremen.[77]

[66] Steamship Minutes May 1957 p. 186
[67] Mr Dhanki email to H Doe
[68] Comment James Stockdale May 2009
[69] Steamship Minutes May 1957 pp. 194-95
[70] Steamship Minutes p. 112
[71] Steamship Minutes p. 201
[72] Sailing Ship Circulars book – Steamship letter 24th April 1939

[73] Steamship Minutes 1956
[74] Steamship Minutes 1955 p. 160
[75] Steamship Minutes 21st January 1959
[76] Steamship Minutes Feb 1958, pp. 204-5
[77] Steamship Minutes 20th Jan 1960, p. 248; 1960 Rule books for Britannia, British Marine, Liverpool & London, London Steamship, Neptune, Newcastle, North of England, Standard, Sunderland, UK, West of England

Chapter 4

MANAGEMENT CHANGE

The 1960s and 1970s see profound changes.
Continued growth and the increasing complexity of the P&I world
result in the Club's move from London to Bermuda and the Managers'
organisational transformation.

By 1960 Steamship Mutual was an established international Club and this was reflected in its Committee members, who now met at 18 London Street. At a time when most of the other mutuals had predominantly British based Committee members, seven of the eleven men on the Steamship Committee were non-British based and their ages ranged from an impressive 95 to a young 35.[1]

There was to be another addition to the Board. David Clarabut was the last Chairman of Sailing Ship, which by now was barge business only, and it was finally wound up in 1964. In his words,

> *The sailing barge entries had become a bit of an anachronism and tonnage entered substantially declined. Coupled with this British [Marine] Mutual and Shipowners were concentrating on the smaller tonnage and with Steamship going for the larger vessels it was inevitable that the time would come when Sailing Ship was no longer a viable proposition.*[2]

Vasant Sheth, Great Eastern
Shipping Company Ltd

C F Ahrenkiel, C F Ahrenkiel
Shipping

Sandy Struthers,
J & A Gardner Ltd

Table 1 : Companies House information on the Directors in 1964

Name	Occupation	Appointed	Age in 1964
Conte Salvatore Tagliavia	Shipowner of Palermo	1952	95
Signor Achille Lauro	Shipowner of Naples	1952	77
Signor Ernesto Fassio	Levante	1954	71
Thomas J Metcalf	Metcalf Motors	1950	65
Christian Ahrenkiel	Shipowner Hamburg	1963	60
Norman Leighton	Stelp and Leighton	1952	50
Dr. Kurt von Laun	Bremen	1955	46
Chandrika P. Srivastava	Managing Dir, The Shipping Corporation of India Ltd, Bombay	1962	44
Peter Dorey	Guernsey	1955	37
Vasant Sheth	Great Eastern	1960	37
Alastair Struthers	Chairman, J & A Gardner & Co Ltd, Glasgow	1963	35

The Shipping World

The annual report from Lloyd's Register of Shipping in 1960 referred to the shipbuilding recession over the previous three years and noted the considerable changes in flag registration. Norwegian owners now had a very significant fleet and had displaced Liberia in scale as Liberia's post-war expansion in shipowning 'has been halted during the past two years by a sensational volume of transfers of existing ships from Liberian to Greek registration in a surge of national feeling which is now being carried forward in the ordering of new tonnage. This Greek movement has also affected Panama, while Honduras and Costa Rica have entirely ceased to attract new registration'.[3]

Flags of convenience (FOC) were not a new concept as shipowners have long used the flexibility of their assets to move to other countries. In the nineteenth century a Westcountry shipowner took great exception to the new legislation being proposed by Plimsoll. In September 1875 they wrote a furious letter to the local shipping registration authorities protesting about new requirements:

> *... in consequence of legislation forced on the Country by the lying misstatements of a man like Plimsoll & we believe if the United States Government were just now to relax the stringency of their laws affecting the transfer of ships to their flag, that in a very short space of time they would have such a merchant navy as they never hitherto possessed.*

[1] 1960 Rule books for Britannia, British Marine, Liverpool & London, London Steamship, Neptune, Newcastle, North of England, Standard, Sunderland, UK, West of England.

[2] David Clarabut to David Hooper, 11th August 1999
[3] *Lloyd's Register of Shipping Annual Report* 1960, p. 93

The letter was written by John Holman and Sons of 23 St Mary Axe, London and of Topsham, Devon who established one of the first P&I Clubs, the West of England Club.[4] It was, however in the twentieth century that FOCs became a thorny issue.[5] Aware of the changing nature of flag registration the Committee of Steamship was considering the analysis of the records of ships under various flags in 1959.[6] The big challenge for shipowners and for P&I was the tough stance taken by the International Transport Workers' Federation (ITWF), which was organising boycotts of FOC ships in protest over the different and less stringent laws that affected the seamen's working conditions and contracts.

The world economy was growing and the reindustrialisation of Japan was a big factor in this period. In North America the focus of growth moved from the Great Lakes to the Pacific coast and the rise of Hong Kong, Taiwan, South Korea and Singapore generated additional trade in the 1970s. In Europe a new order was apparent as former colonial countries such as the Netherlands, Belgium, France and Britain became more focussed on European trade rather than connections with their previous overseas colonies. The demand for minerals increased with ore and coal exports from Brazil, West Africa and North America and oilfields opened in the North Sea to add to supplies from the Middle East.[7]

The Changing World of Shipping: Containerisation

In 1967 another major change to shipping was noted by the Committee when Mr Ahrenkiel requested a briefing document on container traffic.[8] Containerisation had a major impact on liner shipping and 'transformed liner shipping from a stagnating industry at the very limits of its technological capacity into a transport system of almost unlimited dynamism'.

> *The most prominent innovations of containerisation include dramatically new designs for vessels and cargo handling facilities, global door-to-door traffic, early use of computers and the internet, and structural change in the industry through the formation of consortia, alliances and international mega-mergers. This growth was accompanied by significant diversification and projection of power ashore into container terminals, shipping agencies and inland transport. Finally through the creation of global networks, enlargement of scale and worldwide investments by both shipping and port management companies, the container industry, from being a helpmate to globalisation, became one of its major exponents.* [9]

It was a system that removed many claims as petty pilfering became a thing of the past and it was claimed that insurance costs were now lower due to safety from damage and the reduction in pilferage. But it was still a new concept and lessons had to be learnt about the safe stowage of containers on ships and the problems of shifting cargoes.[10] There was now the seamless movement of containers from one destination to another, sometimes well inland. In 1969 P&I cover was extended to include through transit and container liabilities.[11]

Factors affecting Claims

The headline news around the world in 1967 was the loss of the *Torrey Canyon*. This tragedy involving a super tanker and its load of 12,00,000 tons of crude oil had an enormous impact on P&I as owners were held liable for oil pollution and the principle of 'the polluter pays' was brought home to Clubs. Circulars were sent out to all members as the situation unfolded.[12] The US regulations were particularly tough and the P&I Clubs now had to work with TOVALOP (Tanker Owners' Voluntary Agreement concerning Liability for Oil Pollution) to ensure that rules of both the Agreement and the Clubs were compatible. By April 1969 cover was extended to include the TOVALOP liabilities.[13]

Another area of changing practice was more subtle. On many ships, wives and sometimes children of officers were on board and shipowners provided free passage for them. In these cases a letter of indemnity was required to waive claims for them and a separate insurance at Lloyd's was offered to the officer at his expense. In practice such separate claims were very small and it was noted that some other Clubs were now more liberal on the issue so Steamship decided to offer medical and repatriation expenses, excluding those 'expenses consequent on pregnancy'.[14]

Sloman Traveller, built 1984, 7,947 grt, Sloman Neptun Schiffarts AG

[4] Devon Record Office: 3289s/9 Exeter Shipping Register, 3rd September 1875

[5] F Broeze, *The Globalisation of the Oceans: Containerisation from the 1950s to the Present* (St John's, Newfoundland: IMEHA, 2002), p. 217 fwd

[6] Steamship Minutes January 1959

[7] A D Couper, 'Introduction' in Gardiner, Robert (ed) *The Shipping Revolution:The Modern Merchant Ship* (Bath; Conway Maritime Press, 1992), p. 9

[8] Steamship Minutes September 1967

[9] F Broeze, *The Globalisation of the Oceans: Containerisation from the 1950s to the Present* (St John's, Newfoundland: IMEHA, 2002)

[10] W J Young, 'Containerisation – Panacea or White Elephant?', *Fairplay* 9th Feb 1967

[11] Steamship Minutes 22nd September 1969

[12] Steamship Minutes 22nd September 1969

[13] Steamship Minutes April 1969

[14] Steamship Minutes 22nd June 1971

Threat to Expansion

The Italian entries had been a large part of Steamship's growth but in 1967 events in Italy threatened the whole of that business. The Levante company of Genoa had been the main driver of business and although owned by Ernesto Fassio the insurance business was run by his brother Ugo Fassio. A major disagreement arose between the two brothers and Ugo indicated to Steamship that he was preparing to leave Levante and set up his own business. This placed the Club in a difficult position, caught as they were in the cross fire. A briefing document was prepared for the Committee and after some discussion the Committee agreed to appoint Mr Ugo Fassio as Club representative if he were to break away from Levante. Ugo was the key contact and it must be assumed that soundings had been taken by the managers from some Italian owners as to their intentions in the event of such a change. The Committee nevertheless 'hoped that it would be possible to retain the Fassio Line business from Mr Ernesto Fassio if the latter chose to come directly to the club'.[15]

But it was not going to be that easy as Ernesto, who was the official Committee member (despite never having attended a meeting) sent a proxy, Commander Barbaro. He also sent a five page typed memo to the Committee as he was determined to retain the Club's business in Italy. Howard Morgan for the Managers gave his opinion that 'in the event of any dispute between the Fassio brothers the Association must lose some business because of divided loyalties'. The link with the Fassio brothers related to twenty years of good business. With reluctance the Committee agreed to terminate the Levante contract. The Chairman, Norman Leighton, stated that in view of the 'very pleasant relations with the Levante company which had existed over the years they would like to conclude the agreement as amicably as possible'.[16] Subsequently Ernesto withdrew the Villain and Fassio ships and entered them with the Oceanus Club.[17]

> In the event Ugo persuaded Italian shipowners to subscribe 50 per cent of the capital of the new company, and the Chairman of Fiat, Gianni Agnelli, agreed to provide the remaining 50 per cent. The new company, SIAT, became a subsidiary of Fiat. SIAT soon obtained the transfer of most of the Italian Hull business.[18]

Irpinia (ex *Campana*, ex *Rio Jachal*), passenger liner built in 1929, Sicula Oceanica SA (Armatore Grimaldi Fratelli, Managers) at Southampton in 1973

The dispute, into which Steamship had been reluctantly drawn, did not finally end until February 1972 after the death of the two brothers and their estates agreed to settle with Steamship by mutual agreement with just the costs of legal fees to each party.[19]

Ugo's position as managing director of SIAT was filled by his co-director Giorgio Mitolo who had been a close friend and supporter of the Club for many years. Since replacing Levante in 1967 SIAT has continued to act as general agents for the Club in Italy.[20]

Office Space

The growth of the Club necessitated an increase in staff and by 1957, although extra space had been rented at 49 Leadenhall Street, more space was needed. Howard Morgan recalled the situation regarding what he called the 'first move', which was true from his experience but it was in fact the second move for Steamship as the first office had been at 4–5 Lime Street Square.

A new building, the Institute of Marine Engineers' War Memorial building, was being built opposite Fenchurch Street station and was due to be completed by the end of the year. These were attractive offices in a convenient location but the landlords were demanding a rent of £1.25 per square foot. This figure looks deceptively cheap but it was in fact double the rent being paid at 49 Leadenhall Street – added to which we were asked to sign a 20 years unbroken lease! After some hesitation the Club agreed. At that time we were not to know that 15 years hence the market rate for that accommodation would be 630 per cent greater than we had just agreed to pay. Over the coming years we were to take additional space in the Marine Engineers building but fortunately the floors were adjacent.[21]

By 1968 this new accommodation was strained as the employees now numbered 65 and there were plans to increase to 75.[22]

The Banker

With the increased size of the Club its finances were over £2 million by December 1960 and investments were spread widely, with help on occasion of Committee members such as 'Arrangements made through Dr von Laun for the investment of approx £10,000 in German securities'. Equities now comprised about 20 per cent of the total investment.[23] The funds needed to keep pace with growing tonnage as more and bigger ships were entered. A wide variety of investments were made such as Funding Stock, Savings Stock,

[15] Steamship Minutes February 1967
[16] Steamship Minutes February 1967
[17] Steamship Minutes February 1968
[18] Morgan, SSM History draft
[19] Steamship Minutes February 1972
[20] Morgan, SSM History draft
[21] Morgan, SSM History draft
[22] Steamship Minutes 1968
[23] Steamship Minutes 13th December 1960, 28th February 1961

Commonwealth of Australia Stock and shares in two Dutch Investment Trusts. These had been recommended by Mr Abel and approved by the investment brokers. 'These Trusts, being based in Holland, had investments throughout Europe and would provide the Association with an interest in firms participating in the Common Market.'

In 1961 the Club almost became an unofficial bank for the then cash-strapped public sector when it made two loans to local authorities, £130,000 to the Borough of Walthamstow and £100,000 to the City of Leeds. Both were on seven days notice at 5 ¼ per cent. Just a few months later the Investment sub committee decided to realise these loans and so this brief foray into local government lending came to an end.[24]

From time to time requests came from members seeking to raise funds for ship purchases, but these were normally declined as it 'would be undesirable to invest in ship mortgages even if supplemented by additional security and, further, such mortgages would create difficulties for the Committee in the future'. This stance was challenged when a £30,000 loan was agreed for the Merchant Steam Navigation Company in Bombay. The company had been 'esteemed members since 1947' and owned five ships. The need arose due to a shortage of sterling balances in India and the Indian Government would only allow ships to be purchased from non-Indian earnings. The purchase price of the vessel was estimated between £75,000 and £90,000 and the balance was to be provided by an Indian bank and a German shipbroker. The Managers had consulted with Mr. Metcalf, Mr Leighton and Mr Vere da Silva (proxy for Mr Sheth) who was familiar with the subject. Mr da Silva had drafted an agreement for the Club under which the loan would be covered by a deposit in Bombay of 120 per cent of the rupee equivalent. The repayment of the loan would be from non-Indian earnings and expected to be made in three years with interest at 6 per cent per annum free of Indian tax as wages, insurance, fuel, stores and other disbursements would not be deducted from earnings. A guarantee that the loan and interest would be paid in seven years would be given by the Indian Government Authority who would also approve the other terms of the loan. With some hesitation Mr Metcalf had agreed and also Mr Leighton and Mr da Silva. After considerable discussion the rest of the Committee agreed, but in the end the ship was never purchased and the loan was never made. [25]

Before the rift between the two Fassio brothers a loan was requested by them to purchase their leased building. The Villain and Fassio building in Genoa was built in 1954/55 at a cost of £1 million and was now estimated to be worth double that. A letter was received from Ugo Fassio on the morning of a Committee meeting proposing that Steamship provide a loan of £200,000 for the intended purchase price of £1.5 million. Repayment was offered at £50,000 per annum plus reasonable interest. Sydney Crowe said that he had not had time to examine the letter in detail but was inclined to recommend a loan at 6 per cent as the 'business secured from Italian Shipowners by Levante was now 2 million tons with excellent results'. After some debate the loan was agreed but with some collateral security, presumably by a mortgage on the building.

The Committee was congratulatory in September 1966 when the Club's investments were reported at £4.8 million. A situation they were very pleased with in view of the recent recession and they 'especially congratulated Mr Dorey who had staunchly advocated investment in Canadian stock'.[26] The amounts were rising rapidly as just two years later investments were over £6.8 million.[27]

Claims

Higher investment returns were needed to provide for the ever increasing size of claims. A report in 1967 showed that accidents involving death or injury to crew, stevedores, dock workers and others remained responsible for a larger percentage of the calls on members of clubs. The claims of dockers and stevedores in the United States were described as both 'numerous and expensive'.[28] The DG Neptun Line of Bremen were involved in a claim relating to an injury in 1959 where the action had commenced for the sum of $650,000 but the view was that the claim would probably be reduced to $350,000 for which bail was asked and it was estimated that settlement might be obtained at $150,000. The Managers informed the Committee that 'No Neptun Line ships were now going to the USA'.[29] In the case of the *Argea Prima*, a class action was threatened in the sum of $100 million, which in the 'opinion of Mr Burns in New York (agent) was a gross exaggeration'.[30]

Dangerous cargoes mentioned included contamination from tetraethyl lead (a petrol additive) and Australian stevedores requiring extra indemnities from nuclear risks.[31] Meetings were held with the relevant atomic authorities to get guidance in the handling of such cargoes. Under manning and the certification of officers was another concern and Mr Ahrenkiel raised the whole matter of manning as he pointed to the 'second case where the Managers had reported serious claims which had disclosed the failure of owners to apply for permission to use uncertificated officers'. The decision was made to draft a circular on this for members, but the drafting proved problematic and after several attempts to get an agreed draft it was eventually decided to leave it and deal with each case on an individual basis.[32]

Circulars, which had been used since the beginning of the Club to inform members, were sent as lessons were learnt, but some cases just seemed to repeat themselves with tragic consequences. The *Cisterna No 6* explosion in a Venice shipyard was similar to that of the *Montallegro*. Three people were killed and seven injured when fumes in a tank were ignited by an oxy-acetylene torch. Damage was also caused to shore properties. Some claims made case law such as a 1963 tanker collision in the Scheldt. This was a serious collision in fog and involved three tankers. The 20,776 grt tanker *Miraflores* collided with the British tanker *Abadesa* on 26th February 1963. Both tankers caught fire and eight members of the crew of the *Miraflores* were reported missing. The remainder of the crew had to leave the ship which was subsequently brought in by salvors and was heavily damaged. The Club's immediate claims were concerned with the loss of life and injury

[24] Steamship Minutes 25th April 1961, June 1961, 26th September 1961
[25] Steamship Minutes 3rd September 1963
[26] Steamship Minutes September 1965
[27] Steamship Minutes September 1968

[28] *Fairplay*, 12th January 1967
[29] Steamship Minutes 21st July 1959
[30] Steamship Minutes 1961
[31] Steamship Minutes 13th December 1960
[32] Steamship Minutes May 1964

claims, loss of effects, repatriation and shipwreck employment indemnity. There was also another claim from the Panamanian tanker *George Livanos* which grounded after apparently taking avoiding action. This claim from the owners of the *George Livanos* was in the region of $75,000. This case eventually ended up on Appeal to the House of Lords.[33]

The case of the *Ems Ore*, on 1st October 1966 was rather different. While sailing off the English coast, three drunken sailors attempted a mutiny and tried to destroy the ship with an axe and hammers before they were subdued and arrested.[34] Political events caught out another ship, the *Observer*, when, owing to an engine fault, she was not able to get out of the Suez Canal before it was closed in 1967 during the war with Israel and was detained in the Great Bitter Lake. Three other British ships were also trapped in the Great Bitter Lake and the UK Chamber of Shipping raised concerns over the welfare of the crews left on board. The closure of the canal lasted until 1975 and one impact of the route change necessitated by the closure, was the increase in size of oil tankers. The Cape diversion added six to eight days to the Far East voyage time and the cost was multiplied by the rising cost of fuel. The supertanker, no longer restricted by the size limitations of the canal, came into being.[35]

> In 1950 few tankers exceeded 30,000 dwt, but seven years later, after the first
> Suez crisis, almost half the tanker tonnage on order consisted of vessels over this
> threshold. The second closure of the Suez Canal had similar effects; the average size
> of tankers on order increased from approximately 63,000 dwt in 1965 to more than
> 160,000 by 1973.[36]

The physical condition of one ship provoked some rare minuted criticism of the managers by the Committee. The *Tradeways II* had sunk and the Committee was particularly concerned with the physical condition of the vessel and its acceptance by the managers as a risk. The managers were instructed to be selective in their approach to such vessels and in any case to limit their liabilities on them if acceptable. Subsequently Steamship, together with the other insurers, attempted unsuccessfully to sue Bureau Veritas.[37]

The Committee did not hold back from criticism of owners either when it came to the case of the *Nicolaw*. This was owned by William Brandt's (Leasing) Ltd and demise chartered to James Riddell & Sons Ltd. The vessel sank off Boulogne on 16th November 1969 with the loss of life of the master, Mr Wharton, and her cook. The enquiry found that the loss was attributable to the unseaworthy condition at time of sailing to which Mr Wharton both as master and as a director of James Riddell & Sons Ltd was privy. The Directors of James Riddell and Sons wrote to the Committee and placed all the blame on the deceased master, Wharton.

> ...this Board was wholly deceived by Mr Wharton on whom it relied, and in course of
> the dealings at the time had no reason to suspect. They were of course, not alone in
> this as he also succeeded in deceiving various other parties.

The Committee rejected the claims from Riddle, but the managers were requested to advise the owners, William Brandt's (Leasing) Ltd, of the 'feeling of the Committee regarding the situation' and that although cover would not be withheld them as owners of *Nicolaw* 'it was not considered that an owner could divest himself of all responsibilities'.[38]

The Club in 1967

In a *Fairplay* article on P&I the various Clubs emphasised their strengths and it is interesting to note how each Club represented itself in the short space that was allowed. The UK Club promoted its size as 'The largest P&I Association in the world, its shipowner members coming from nearly 70 countries and own some 34,000,000 tons gross shipping'. The West of England had 4,200 vessels entered with a total tonnage of 20 million and they emphasised the type of claims they handled. The North of England Club with 1.6 million entered tonnage highlighted its pedigree as one of the oldest of its kind. Skuld emphasised that its 17 million tons included both Scandinavian and Continental shipping. While Steamship, the youngest club, decided to feature its international credentials with 6 million tons entered 'from all the principal maritime nations with appropriate representation on the Club Committee'. In addition, it added, the 'Club rules have been published in German, Italian and Spanish'.[39]

Senior Management Change

New technology began to make an appearance. A Committee member, Peter Dorey, asked in 1963 if the Association had considered installing telex 'as an aid to efficiency'. The reply from Sydney Crowe was that the matter had been considered, but no action taken, but 'in view of the Committee's obvious approval he undertook to see whether one could be installed without delay'. In December that year the installation was duly reported.[40] Just five years later the managers submitted a short memo regarding 'a programme now being considered for computerisation of members' calls and claims statistics'. This they hoped to have ready for operation by 29 February 1969.[41]

In September 1970 the Committee chairman, Sandy Struthers, informed the meeting that although 'Mr Crowe was retiring on 30th September he would be a regular attendee at Committee meetings and available as consultant and the Committee would always be pleased to see him'. After 37 years with the Club Sydney Crowe was stepping back from his leading position but was not entirely letting go of the organisation he had done so much to develop. J F L Morton was appointed Secretary to the Committee in his place and Howard Morgan took over as senior manager.[42]

[33] Steamship Minutes 1963
[34] Steamship Minutes 1968
[35] *Fairplay* 3rd August 1967
[36] Stig Tenold, *Tankers in Trouble: Norwegian Shipping and the Crisis of the 1970s and 1980s* (St John's, Newfoundland: IMEHA, 2006), pp. 12-13
[37] Steamship Minutes 1968
[38] Steamship Minutes 2nd March 1971
[39] *Fairplay* 21st September 1967
[40] Steamship Minutes 3rd December 1963
[41] Steamship Minutes 1968
[42] Steamship Minutes 22nd September 1970

Sydney Crowe

Sydney was born in 1906 in Kingston upon Thames. His father was a house painter but both his parents died young and Sydney and his two sisters were effectively brought up by their older sister Ivy. Without private financial support Sydney's formal schooling finished at the age of 14 and he started work in the City working for William Richards & Son who were average adjusters. He continued to educate himself by attending evening classes and as he was both bright and determined he won prizes. In his view, if the prize was a book he applied or if the prize was money he bought more books.

In 1921 at the age of 15 he successfully completed the General Commercial Education Certificate of the London Chamber of Commerce and gained distinctions in three of the four subjects; bookkeeping, shorthand speed (80 words per minute) and typewriting. His secretary Doreen, who spent many hours taking dictation from him in the 1950s, never knew that her boss was so skilled.

By 1932 Sydney had taken his Chartered Insurance Institute examinations passing Marine Branch Part 1 with honours in the principles and practice of insurance, general average (York Antwerp rules), shipping and mercantile practice, history and organisation. In part II the next year he gained honours again in general average, law and accounts. His success was recognised by the Institute of London Underwriters who awarded one of the two annual prizes to him. He was a man of great determination and this was demonstrated in 1930 when, at the age of 25, he and his fellow oarsman, aged 45, won the long distance double sculling championship on the Thames. This skiff race started from Putney Bridge and finished at Richmond Lock, a distance of eight and a half miles. At the end they put on a final spurt and won the race by just two feet and made a new record of 55 minutes, beating the old record by seven minutes. After his retirement he took an interest in horse racing and invested in race horses with Ravi Tikkoo. One year their horse, *Steel Pulse,* won the Irish Derby and Sandy Struthers, a long standing Committee member and Chairman, saw his horse, *Scottish Rival,* beaten into second place.[43]

Sydney Crowe and partner winning the marathon skiff race in 1930

Sydney Crowe was known as a man who could do every job within the organisation and he personally read every piece of post coming in to the business. His all encompassing knowledge probably made the possibilities of progression frustrating for those close to him in seniority, but for most of his staff he was a much admired figure. Howard Morgan, his successor, described him as a man with many fine qualities who had 'a fine brain, a real sense of humour, and tremendous compassion – especially for the underdog. No one was ever sacked for inability to cope. Some suitable niche was found to help everybody. The only sure way to incur Sydney's displeasure was to offend against the moral code'.[44]

A New Senior Partner

Howard Morgan took over at a difficult time. For a while there had been problems with international currencies. The claims currency was the pound sterling which was under severe pressure and in 1967 it had been devalued by 14 per cent by the Wilson Government. This shrinking pound caused real difficulties in an international Club.[45]

At one Committee meeting the Chairman, Christian Ahrenkiel, commented on the current difficulties facing shipowners 'not the least of which included competition from the Russian state aided fleets and he particularly drew the attention of the Committee to the need for preservation of the funds of the association in case of currency difficulties'. Funds were held in Deutsche marks and lire and permission was being sought for Swiss francs. If possible the Club needed to build these accounts up substantially to provide a partial hedge against devaluation.[46] The Exchange Control Regulations were 'the greatest drawback to a successful preservation of equity'. Another challenge was the tax situation. Even though the Club was non-profit making Corporation Tax was charged on dividends, interest and capital gains on investments. The Club's assets belonged in the main to non-resident members as 70 per cent were non-resident in the sterling area. For the first time consideration was given to forming a new Club outside the United Kingdom and it was known that other British based clubs were considering this also. In 1968 a subsidiary was set up in the Bahamas as a holding position and a subsidiary in Guernsey was also considered.[47]

[43] A Struthers 6th April 2009
[44] H Morgan Tribute to S Crowe 1986
[45] Morgan, SSM History draft

[46] Steamship Minutes December 1968
[47] Steamship Minutes June 1968

Common Market Impact

In December 1972 came further mention of the Common Market (the popular term for the European Economic Community) and the P&I Clubs.[48] The European Economic Community (EEC) was founded in 1957 and the first six countries were France, West Germany, Italy and the three Benelux countries: Belgium, the Netherlands and Luxembourg. Now however, Denmark, Ireland and the United Kingdom were about to join. Greece, Spain and Portugal joined throughout the 1980s and with the creation of the European Union (EU) in 1993, it was enlarged to include a further fifteen countries by 2007.

This was a concern for organisations such as the P&I Clubs as the EEC had strict rules on what they saw as cartels. Discussions were ongoing with the British Department of Trade and Industry who had been negotiating with the EEC authorities and they took the line that the mutual associations were 'better safeguarded by complying with [the European] directive's provision rather than by 'buying time' through temporary exemption in hope of getting the Directive changed'.[49] In other words, in the view of the British civil servants, the Clubs had little chance of changing the EEC's position. This was the beginning of a long campaign by the Clubs to educate the relevant authorities about the mutual system.

It was not just in Europe that the Club needed to be aware of changing legislation as the Indian Government nationalised insurance and there were plans for P&I to be nationalised by 1974. Steamship covered most of the shipping in India (except the Shipping Corporation of India which at that time had gone to a new Club, Oceanus) and Howard Morgan headed for India to investigate the situation.

Business Expansion Continues

Through this the work of the Club continued, if one part of the world was in conflict then other parts of the world were expanding.

> *Throughout the 60s the Club tonnage continued to expand but the 'core' tonnage comprised mainly the big blocks of German, Indian and Italian vessels. Towards the end of the decade the Managers increasingly felt the desirability of a better world-wide spread despite the fact that by 1970 the overall tonnage had increased to 7 million grt. Some measure of success was achieved in the Far East and Brazil. In Brazil the Club was assisted by an influential broker [Horacio Milliet] in Rio de Janeiro. His introductions resulted in the entry of a large block of ocean going Brazilian tonnage. Some of this tonnage was previously uninsured for P&I – a fact which made initial rating difficult. Some years later when a substantial increase in final calls was necessary the extra cost was in part due to the under-rating of Brazilian business. Brazilian vessels were, of course, only one factor.[50]*

In December 1970 the Managers suggested that a least one of the four annual Committee meetings should be held abroad so that the Committee had the opportunity to meet more of the Club's members and, in June 1971, a meeting was held in Genoa.

In 1970 the Managers organised the first Committee luncheon on a meeting day. For many years the Committee Meetings started only at 2.30 p.m. and were normally completed by 5.30 p.m. However, times were changing and it was not long before the business required meetings to start earlier in the day. In June 1971 the Club held its first Committee Meeting outside the UK. The meeting was held in Genoa in the 'Golden Room' of the Genoa Chamber of Commerce. The occasion was featured in the Genoa press and was followed by a large reception and dinner for Italian shipowners and their ladies at Portofino. The Club was indebted to Mr. Cameli for his kindness in hosting a pre-dinner cocktail party at his summer residence. The Genoa event was so successful that it was decided to hold a similar event in Hamburg in June 1973. We were indebted to Mr. Christian F. Ahrenkiel for hosting the pre-dinner cocktail party at his house in Blankanese. At the subsequent dinner in Hamburg

The Board in Genoa, June 1971. From left to right: Juergen Willhoeft, Ardavast Postyan, David Clarabut, Leonidas Valmas, Sydney Crowe, Alan Tolhurst, Howard Morgan, Alastair Struthers, Julian Morton (Company Secretary), Christian Ahrenkiel snr, Peter Dorey

48 Steamship Minutes 5th December 1972
49 Steamship Minutes June 1973
50 Morgan, SSM History draft

the Club Chairman made a speech in German. Howard Morgan was permitted to propose a toast to 'The Ladies' in English – having promised not to speak Welsh.[51]

A further change came in 1971 when the Committee discussed the question of inviting important owners and brokers to join the Committee luncheon from time to time and an invitation was extended to the Managing Director of Kuwaiti Oil Tanker (UK) Ltd.[52] He subsequently joined the Club and the Committee.

Committee Management

The increasing numbers of claims were making the work of the claims committee onerous. This sub committee was made up of two Committee members who reviewed claims, usually before the main meeting, but there was little time to view more than one or two of the now more complex claims. In 1964 it was decided to look at an alternative method and so the sub committee was discontinued. Now a list of claims over £2,000 was to be circulated and the reporting was restricted to new claims over £5,000, material changes in claims over £5,000 previously reported, claims submitted for the Committee decision and claims of 'novel or particular interest'.[53] How to handle the proper review of claims was to be a constant concern as claims increased in size, number and complexity. By 1971 the claims sub committee was re-established, but by 1974 the Chairman advised the Committee that the increase in tonnage might well 'cause an increase of up to two hundred more pages in the claims report'.[54] So now only claims in excess of £25,000 were to be reported except cases of special interest or involving matters of principle. An independent audit of the claims was suggested as there were around 10,000 to 15,000 files containing up to 100,000 claims. An independent maritime lawyer was proposed but after some debate the claims sub committee approached Sydney Crowe, who was acting as a consultant to the Club. He naturally expressed concern about this considering his relationship with the Managers, but it was eventually agreed he would select 300 files at random and then report to the Managers who would report to the Committee. The Chairman, David Clarabut, was at pains to emphasise that this was not a criticism of the claims handling but a need for the Committee to discharge their duty 'in view of the large amounts'.[55]

Increased claims led to supplementary calls and these always carried a risk of loss of members and the Indian market was of some concern, but a strong relationship with the Club's Indian agents, Crowe Boda, mitigated the risk.

Another important event was when Steamship Mutual ordered huge supplementary calls during the period 1972 to 1975. It was feared that many Indian owners may decide to leave Steamship Mutual. However, Mr J B Boda accepted the challenge of convincing all the Indian members to remain with Steamship Mutual and, for this purpose, he requested Mr Howard Morgan and Mr Sydney Crowe who was then acting as a Consultant to the Club to make a special trip to India and fully explain their position to all the members. A meeting was convened in the Ambassador Hotel in Mumbai and, after marathon discussions, the situation could be salvaged and

*all the members gave their wholehearted support and continued the entry of their
vessels with Steamship Mutual. It may be mentioned that, during this whole exercise,
the Club also received excellent support from some of the senior executives of Indian
shipping companies such as Mr F G Dastur of South India Shipping, Mr Vasant Sheth
of Great Eastern and also Captain J C Anand of India Steamship.*

One member who was co-opted to the Finance sub committee in 1969 was Ravi
Tikkoo.[56] Ravi was an Indian entrepreneur who in 1967, at the age of 40, founded Globtik
Tankers with $2,500 after three years of working in London as a middleman between
shipowners and bankers. When *Globtik Tokyo* was launched in Japan it was, at 238,232 grt,
the largest supertanker in the world at that time and remained the largest for many years.
Subsequently the largest tanker in the twentieth century was the *Seawise Giant,* 238,558
grt, owned by C Y Tung of OOCL and this was also insured with Steamship Mutual.

Significant Claims

In 1988 in an article for *Lloyd's List*, Steamship Mutual outlined the high level of personal
injury awards, particularly those in the US. The Jones Act was highlighted, which was an
act that applied to seamen, a widely defined term, who could claim for negligence from
their employers.[57] A particular case was that of Pires.

*Pires, a 22 year old Brazilian national, was serving on board the 'Frotaleste', a
Brazilian flag vessel, as a wiper in the engine room under a standard Brazilian
seaman's employment contract when the vessel docked at the port of Galveston on
11th December 1975. That evening Pires went ashore with three other crewmen
in order to phone home having, it is alleged, requested directions through the port
area from one of the ship's officers. Whilst crossing the darkened port area Pires was
struck by a railway truck, which moved without warning, and severely injured his right
leg. Pires was then taken to hospital where his leg was amputated above the knee.*

Initially the Club assisted Pires in claiming from the Port Authorities but an American
lawyer advised him to sue his employer under the Jones Act. The case dragged on and by
1989 figures in the region of $31 million were being discussed.[58] The case has yet to be
finally concluded.

In August 1974 the *Oranjeland* ran aground on rocks off East London, South Africa in strong
gales. The wreck remained stuck on the rocks and became quite a tourist attraction for the
area. Eventually it was dismantled to five metres below the water and the ship's almost new
bridge equipment was donated to the General Botha Training Station at Simon's Town in 1976.[59]

[51] Morgan, SSM History draft
[52] Steamship Minutes 21st September 1971
[53] Steamship Minutes December 1964
[54] Steamship Minutes 12th March 1974
[55] Steamship Mutual (Bermuda) 8th October 1974

[56] Steamship Minutes 22nd September 1969
[57] *Lloyd's List* 7th January 1988
[58] Steamship Mutual (Bermuda) 19th September 1989
[59] Margaret Webb 10th April 2009

Business Changes

The American small craft business had been underwritten on a modest scale for some years (see Chapter 3), but this was gradually extended to cover the whole of the US coastline and Canada. It covered many different types of small craft involved in supply, pilotage and support for oil exploration. It was a specialised market and Steamship had gained additional ocean going tonnage for the main mutual business. In 1972 Clifford Parr, a Manager, who had been with Steamship for many years and who specialised in this small craft business decided to set up a new company dedicated to small craft. He left Steamship together with two other staff and the Club decided to cease underwriting this fixed premium business and subsequently referred brokers to Parr's new company.[60] This was the first departure of the older generation (as it was seen by the younger managers) and Parr was replaced by David Staines who moved from claims to underwriting.[61]

The big challenge to shipowners in the 1970s were the oil price shocks of 1973 and 1974 as the Organisation of Petroleum Exporting Countries (OPEC) flexed its muscles. The shipping industry was hit hard and there was a sharp reduction in the growth of demand for tankers.[62] The shipping crisis that followed in the 1970s and 1980s was the most severe depression in shipping of the twentieth century. As the oil crisis impacted the tankers one key lesson was that the Club needed to keep a balance across the different types of tonnage so that it was not overly exposed if one sector went down, however, the shipping depression was to affect all sectors.

Another Office Move

Rents were continuing to increase and it was suggested that it might be wise to buy a suitable property in London.[63] By June 1971 lack of office space was still a problem and exacerbated by the difficulty of finding a suitable property in what was now a booming market. Two suitable buildings were identified but in each case the Club was outbid.[64]

Oranjeland wreck in 1974

Jal Azad, passenger cargo steamer, Scindia Steam Navigation Ltd, in dock in London

The Chairman at the time, Sandy Struthers, suggested a move outside London. This was something that the British Government of the day was keen to promote and several large companies had relocated to places like Swindon, Reading and Portsmouth, but such moves were not always popular with staff. The Managers explained to the Committee that the Club's 'style of organisation would not be helped by separation' of staff in different locations. They added for good measure that it was 'vital to have a central operation near Lloyd's market'.[65] The suggestion of moving outside London did not go away and the Managers were persuaded to look at a site outside London and planning permission was obtained in 1974 in a town 55 miles from the City. But the Managers had second thoughts and this time came up with another reason for not moving. The big difficulty, they explained, was in obtaining staff in the 22-35 age group. The Club had always recruited from other insurance companies in the City and they suspected it would be difficult to tempt them to come to the provinces at their age. To underline the importance of making the right decision they pointed out that the '50 per cent increase in tonnage this year made them very conscious of avoiding making administrative mistakes and they had some doubts regarding staff'.[66]

The Managers and the Committee could afford to be very pleased with progress on the expansion of the Club as it announced in March 1974 that the Club's tonnage as at 20th February 1974 was 17,967,259 compared to 11,890,804 at February 1973. This 51 per cent increase was spread over the whole list with an expanding tanker and bulk carrier business and included the Texaco fleet of 2,800,000 tons.[67]

Office space was now a high priority and the Club was helped by a declining property market in 1974 and a building site in Bishopsgate, adjacent to Liverpool Street station, became available.

> A collapsed property development company wanted to sell the site plus the contract for demolition of the old building and re-building to provide about 20,000 square feet. It seemed an excellent proposition. It was a rare freehold site and the price asked was £2 million for the land plus £900,000 for assignment of the building contract. This time there was no effective competition. The vendors attempted to create the impression that other potential buyers were interested but the Club Managers took a signed contract by taxi to the vendors' offices and exchange was quickly completed. Before the end of 1974 the Club was in occupation; the only London P&I Club to own its own building.[68]

[60] Morgan, SSM History draft
[61] James Stockdale May 2009
[62] For a detailed study see Tenold, *Tankers in Trouble*
[63] Steamship Minutes 22nd September 1969
[64] Morgan, SSM History draft

[65] Steamship Minutes 22nd June 1971
[66] Steamship Minutes 12th March 1974, Steamship Mutual (Bermuda) 8th October 1974
[67] Steamship Minutes 12th March 1974
[68] Morgan, SSM History draft

The Bahamas,
Bermuda and Guernsey

If all this change was not enough Howard Morgan and his colleagues had to deal with the big taxation questions of the day on investments and the continuing currency difficulties. Two Clubs had already set up operations in Bermuda and advice was sought in 1965 on the possibility of a Bahamas subsidiary, but the Committee 'wished to be satisfied that Treasury or Revenue sanction was obtained'. After being reassured on the matter a subsidiary was duly set up, but by 1970 due to a change of government in the Bahamas there were concerns over stability and so shell companies were established in both Bermuda and Guernsey as prudent alternatives in case of need.[69]

It was not just the Club itself that had to adapt to a changing tax regime in Britain. Before 1965, companies had paid income tax on their income in the same way as individuals. The Finance Act 1965 not only introduced corporation tax but also for the first time imposed a new tax on chargeable gains called capital gains tax. Alfred Stocken and Co Ltd as a limited company was changed to a partnership, which was in effect a better reflection of the nature of that organisation.[70]

It was Howard Morgan who was the key person in much of the offshore debate and he recalled it well:

> Between 1969 and 1974 certain important developments had already taken place in connection with a few other Clubs. Most of the large Clubs had a substantial foreign membership. A West of England Club had been formed in Luxembourg and a United Kingdom Club and a Standard Club had been formed in Bermuda. Clubs based in the United Kingdom were subject to exchange control and to English taxation upon investment income. The Bank of England was helpful in delegating authority to the Club's London bankers to approve modest foreign remittances but many applications had to be made each day. As regards taxation the Club was in competition with the Norwegian Clubs, Skuld and Gard, which paid no tax on investment income because mutuals were exempt under Norwegian law. A further point of concern at this time was the continued depreciation of sterling. It was unattractive to have a depreciating calls currency. English Clubs were prevented, by the provisions of the Taxes Acts, from transferring assets abroad for the purpose of saving tax, but there was nothing to prevent non-UK residents from setting up an entirely new Club anywhere in the world. 95 per cent of the Members of Steamship Mutual were non-UK residents and this was reflected in the predominantly foreign Membership of the Steamship Mutual Committee. In the autumn of 1974 the foreign nationals who were also Members of the Committee of Steamship Mutual, London, gave notice that they intended to instruct Bermuda lawyers to set up a new Club in Bermuda and to appoint new Bermuda Managers to run it. The UK residents who were Members of the SSM London Committee offered no opposition. SSM London later agreed to act as London Representatives of the Bermuda Managers of SSM Bermuda. SSM Bermuda became

Howard Morgan

Hamilton, Bermuda

operational on 20th February 1975 from which time most of the tonnage which had been entered in SSM London transferred to SSM Bermuda. A major exception was the Indian tonnage which did not transfer to Bermuda until 20th February 1976. A Bermuda property company (a subsidiary of SSM Bermuda) acquired the Bishopsgate office building occupied by SSM London. The calls currency of the new Club was, of course, US dollars. All the new offshore Clubs were admitted to the London Group Pool.[71]

Sydney Crowe, who had done so much to lead the Club in its expansion, had now fully retired as the senior partner of Alfred Stocken. The Club was now based in Bermuda (the assets of Bahamas Mutual Insurance Association were transferred to SSM Bermuda in 1971)[72] and dealing was mainly in US dollars. It had a management office in London and a new building. There was a subsidiary in Guernsey, managed by Hambros Bank and in 1972 one was also set up in Hong Kong with Jardine Matheson acting as administrators.[73] The Committee members were now the Directors and the majority were non-British shipowners. Steamship had fully made the transition from a mainly British club to a global organisation.

[69] Steamship Minutes November 1965, 22nd September 1970
[70] Steamship Minutes November 1965
[71] Morgan, SSM History draft

[72] Steamship Minutes 20th August 1971
   Note: This is not the current SMUA Bermuda, which was incorporated in 1974
[73] Steamship Minutes 19th July 1972

Chapter 5

BERMUDA TO TODAY

The 1980s to the present day sees the Club embracing modern corporate governance and risk management in reaction to rising and more complex claims, increasing regulation and the effects of globalisation.

If currency fluctuations had been the big challenge of the 1960s and 1970s, now the challenges came from legislation emerging from the European Union (EEC), the British Inland Revenue, increasing regulatory oversight and the continuing swings of the world wide economy. All of these were set against a backdrop of the end of the Cold War, the collapse of communism, increasing terrorism, wars in many parts of the world, the great consumer boom and the rise of world concern about environmental damage. Ships became yet larger and the world wide economy became ever more integrated.

In July 1980 the Managers reported to the Board that the International Group Clubs had met to finalise a formal agreement for submission to the EEC for ratification.[1] The London Group of Clubs dated back to 1929 when some of the larger clubs came together to agree not to get business by rate cutting. At the time these Clubs had attracted business from the USA and as there was then no experience in the United States market the agreement was important. It was an informal agreement that was eventually formalised in the 1960s, by which time Steamship was a member of the London Group. In 1975 it was realised that such an agreement could potentially infringe the Treaty of Rome so the formal agreement was scrapped. As James Stockdale recalls

> The informal arrangement known as the 'Gentleman's Agreement' came into existence. By that time the three Scandinavia based Clubs, then reinsured into the Group pooling arrangement, were seeking direct membership in their own right. With them joining, the London Group was to metamorphose into the now well known International Group of P&I Clubs. In order to govern the increasingly complex relationships within the Group, it was recognised that a more formal Group Agreement would be required which would necessitate clearance from Brussels.

It was decided that an application should be made to the EEC for approval of what was to become known as the International Group Agreement (IGA). Being mutual non-profit organisations the P&I Clubs were not the targets of the EEC legislators. A new draft agreement had now been produced in which a new Club must request the old Club for such details as claims record and the premium it would ask for renewal. A Rating

Etagas, LPG tanker launched 1988, 7,314 grt, Sloman Neptun Schiffarts AG

Committee would be set up to see if the rate was below the 'holding' Club's rate. Should the Rating Committee decide that the new rate was in breach and the new Club had taken the business, then the new Club would be barred from pooling claims on that business for two years.

There were questions from the Directors relating to the ability to move between the Clubs as shipowners needed to be able to keep their options open and some had split their fleets across two or more Clubs. The view was that such an agreement would not freeze movement between the Clubs since the main ground for differentiation was on service. Additionally, it was pointed out, the old Agreement, which had contained greater support obligations between Clubs, had not stopped transfers from one Club to another.

[1] Steamship Mutual (Bermuda) 22nd July 1980

A new Club could always take the business at any rate if it was prepared to arrange special reinsurance as an alternative to pooling the risk.

All was going well. The EEC seemed to recognise the very different nature of the mutual, non-profit system and in 1982 had indicated that agreement was likely. However in September of that year pressure from the Greek Shipowners' Cooperation Committee (GSCC), a body made up of London-based Greek shipowners who were members of International Group Clubs, made a legal challenge to the Group Agreement. The Greeks wanted more freedom and flexibility within the terms of the IGA. They did not necessarily feel it was wrong in principle, but disagreed with its strict terms.[2] The GSCC were also challenging other aspects of the finance and the management agreements of the Clubs. By 1984 they had commissioned a report from Coopers and Lybrand to examine the practice of the Clubs within the International Group. The resultant report caused uproar as it was highly critical of the Clubs and in Steamship's case included serious inaccuracies. Steamship responded swiftly and Coopers and Lybrand were compelled to withdraw their comments and issue an apology and a rewritten report.[3] After protracted negotiations, by 1985 the European Commission had finally agreed to treat the International Group as exempt from the provision of the Treaty of Rome for ten years until 1995 and the Greek Shipowners' Cooperation Committee offered no further objections. The view from the press was that the 'three-cornered discussions in Brussels, London and Athens have resulted in an increased degree of competition' with rules slightly eased to make the transition between Clubs easier and 'new buildings which constitute a different type of ship for a particular owner are now to be considered as 'free' business'.[4] The information, on what was being built for whom in which shipyard, became of even greater importance to the various clubs.

The other major challenge to the Clubs came from the United Kingdom Inland Revenue Service which was believed to be considering changing the long established concept of company residence for tax purposes, from being based on the location of the company's 'mind and management' and replacing it with the European concept of 'day to day management and control'. In view of the extensive London based operations of a number of Club Managers, this posed a serious challenge as it could have exposed the whole of the Club's investment income to UK tax, which, until that point, had been tax free.

> In 1980 the Revenue's challenge was a conceptual one directed not just at the P&I Clubs. Steamship reacted by creating its Trust structure to move the Club's reserves further away from UK jurisdiction.[5]

Steamship Mutual had been operational in Bermuda since 1975 and was treated as non-resident in the UK. In order to remain competitive it was essential to protect investment income and other Bermuda based Clubs shared this view. Since 1975 all Directors' Meetings were held abroad and all Directors' decisions were taken outside the UK.[6] Expert advice was sought and the result was the setting up of The Steamship Mutual Trust, based on a suggestion by Sudhir Mulji who, at the time, was an alternate member of the Board for Vasant Sheth. To facilitate the change in structure, in 1982 Howard Morgan moved to Bermuda and the approved Managers of Steamship Mutual London

Sudhir Mulji, Great Eastern Shipping Company Ltd

were employed by Steamship Mutual Management (Bermuda) Ltd (SSMB) while working outside the UK. SSMB had been set up in 1979.[7]

The threat of a legislative change in the test for tax residence never materialised but five years later the Inland Revenue were to mount another attack. Up to 1988 the Inland Revenue had 'accepted' the non residence argument but in that year, under pressure from the Treasury to reduce tax avoidance and encouraged by a number of Clubs having, under protest, registered under the 1978 Insurance Companies Act, it determined to tax the mutuals' investment income.[8]

The potential threat required joint representation to the Inland Revenue and the explanation of the unique P&I system to another set of civil servants. The key points in the Bermuda Clubs' case were their non-profit making status, the fact that the overwhelming majority of members were non-British and the substantial foreign income generated for the United Kingdom by their London representatives. Foreign-based Clubs, such as those in Norway were exempt from tax on investment income in their own countries. This gave them a competitive edge as the size of the reserves was an important hedge from future calls for the shipowner. Another concern was that the majority non-UK directors might decide to instruct that the management of the Club be removed from the United Kingdom to a more amenable jurisdiction.[9]

In 1990 the UK and Bermuda based clubs agreed a sector tax settlement with the Inland Revenue which effectively required corporation tax to be paid on 10 per cent of investment income. Steamship, sheltered, amongst other things, by The Steamship Mutual Trust (SMT), only agreed to pay tax on 7.75 per cent of the Club's own investment

[2] *Fairplay* December 1986
[3] Steamship Mutual (Bermuda) 20th March 1985
[4] *Fairplay* December 1986
[5] James Stockdale comment 7th April 2009
[6] Steamship Mutual (Bermuda) 27th July 1982

[7] Steamship Mutual (Bermuda) 19th December 1989, James Stockdale comment 7th April 2009
[8] Steamship Mutual (Bermuda) 19th December 1989, James Stockdale comment 7th April 2009
[9] Steamship Mutual (Bermuda) 17th March 1981, 27th March 1990

income excluding any consideration of its overseas subsidiaries or SMT.[10]

In all of these debates the Club gained considerable benefit from its membership of the International Group of P&I Clubs. The benefit was not just in the access to the larger pool but, as became evident, in being able to respond to national and international challenges backed by the strength and influence of a wider group.[11]

Finance

The problem of currency fluctuation in the 1960s and 1970s had not gone away and, together with the ever increasing importance of investment reserves as the acceptability of unbudgeted supplementary calls diminished, was becoming a topic of debate for the Club's Board. The differing views of the international and knowledgeable Directors on the Finance Committee were evident in debates on investment in currencies with opinions ranging from support for the US dollar as the currency of the future to support for the growing significance of the Japanese yen. Sterling was not seen as a strong currency, although it was supported by at least one German member. These debates also benefitted from input from the Club's professional advisers.[12]

In the deep shipping recession in the early and mid 1980s a close eye once more needed to be kept on debtors and in 1986 the Managers had to admit that the prompt collection of premiums was becoming progressively more difficult even though the overall debt position was no worse than at the same time in 1985.[13]

The next big problem was an escalation in claims, described as devastating by James Stockdale. This was experienced by all the Clubs from the late 1980s.

> During the shipping recession in the earlier part of the '80s, claims had fallen significantly and, combined with the general financial strains faced by shipowners, resulted in considerable downward pressure on premium rates and the extensive rebating of supplementary calls by a number of the Clubs, including Steamship. Over the period from 1986 to 1991, Steamship's claims multiplied. With the relatively primitive statistical projection techniques in use at the time, Steamship, in common with the other Clubs, did not become aware of the scope of the problem until it was too late to deal with it through increases at renewal.[14]

As claims escalated and various clubs announced additional calls for years ranging from 1986 to 1992, Steamship was relatively fortunate in only having to raise calls for 1990 and 1991.[15] Making a call is one of the hardest decisions for any Club and it is made by people, the Directors, who are themselves going to be directly impacted along with the other Club members.

As the extent of the crisis facing the Clubs became apparent, members, potential new members and their brokers put increased pressure on their Managers to supply clearer figures about outstanding incurred and projected claims. Such openness was new to P&I

Cunard celebrated its 150th anniversary in 1990, while a member of Steamship

[10] James Stockdale comment 7th April 2009
[11] Steamship Mutual (Bermuda) 12th July 1977
[12] Steamship Mutual (Bermuda) 1st November 1977
[13] Steamship Mutual (Bermuda) 23rd September 1986
[14] James Stockdale 26th May 2009
[15] Steamship Mutual (Bermuda) 19th September 1989

and the main concern was that such figures could only be estimated by their very nature and, in relation to the most recent years, were regarded by some Managers as highly speculative.[16] Information was duly released and was well received by the industry since it provided reassurance to those concerned about the Club's overall security.[17] By this time the International Group accounting standards required the disclosure of figures, including IBNRs (amounts incurred but not reported), for outstanding claims for all open policy years. In James Stockdale's view this 'can be seen in retrospect as the first milestone in the development of sophisticated reserving techniques and increased levels of transparency which were to transform P&I underwriting over the next two decades'.[18]

Claims

Among the larger claims handled by the Club in the 1970s was one that caught the attention of the press who referred to it as 'The World's Most Expensive Hand Shake'. During the early hours of 16th December 1977 the *Venpet* was on a ballast voyage from Nova Scotia, Canada to Kharg Island in the Persian Gulf to load a new oil cargo – again for Nova Scotia – when she collided with another huge oil carrier – her sister ship the 331,000 dwt *Venoil*, which was coming out from Kharg Island, carrying a load of 307,000 tons of crude oil.[19] They collided with each other in waters off South Africa's Cape St Vincent. Both vessels burst into flames and fortunately the *Venoil*'s cargo did not catch fire but her fuel tanks did. The crews leapt into the water and all but two were rescued. The resultant oil slick was reported as being six miles long and two miles wide. A South African official speculated on the collision suggesting that the vessels had closed in deliberately to allow their crewmen to exchange greetings.[20] The report to the Directors explained that 'contrary to newspaper comments, the vessels were not making a rendezvous but were both steaming at 17 knots in dense fog with zero visibility'. However both masters and the third officers were censured and the third officers were sent on a radar course as both had committed the 'same reciprocal navigation errors'. The cost to the Club was estimated to be $½ million on each ship.[21]

The rising claims pattern did not abate in 1989 and it was also apparent that the Club was being adversely affected by the very high level of fees, particularly in the United States, and claims on the International Group (IG) pool. The *Exxon Valdez* oil spill disaster in Alaska in 1989 was on an even greater scale than the *Torrey Canyon* incident and although not directly insured by Steamship, the Club was inevitably affected as a member of the IG. While the amount of oil spilled may not have been as great as the *Torrey Canyon*, as a claim it was many times larger in terms of financial and political consequences. The most major long term result of the claim was the passing of the US Oil Pollution Act of 1990 (OPA) and the requirement that, initially, every tanker and, subsequently, every commercial vessel trading to the US be issued with a Certificate of Financial Responsibility (COFR). Similarly the *Herald of Free Enterprise* disaster, with the loss of many lives in 1987, although insured by the Standard Club, also had serious implications for Steamship and the other Group clubs both in terms of the cost of contributions to the Pool and, later, the dramatic increase in the cost of the Group Excess Loss Reinsurance contract which was to follow in the 1990s.[22]

MV *William Carson* – lost in ice off Labrador – 3rd June 1977

Despite general improvements in ship safety there were still claims for explosions. One serious claim was due to an explosion and the subsequent sinking of the *Feoso Sun* at Bataan on 7th November 1978. The loss of life was tragic. Eight Chinese and eleven Indonesian crew members were killed, as well as shoreworkers, ten Filipino and one Japanese. A further four crewmembers were hospitalised. The explosives expert sent to Bataan reported that the cause was probably a spark created when a drum of lubricating oil was dropped on deck and such a spark was sufficient to ignite hydrocarbon gases leaking from a cargo tank. The first report to the Directors informed them that the potential liability was unknown but that $1 million might well be needed just for loss of life and the Club could also be responsible for oil pollution and wreck removal.[23]

One claim that came to the Board for special consideration related to the changing view of authorities on the costs of emergency services. In June 1984 the *Tesubu II*, a tanker,

[16] Steamship Mutual (Bermuda) 19th September 1989
[17] Steamship Mutual (Bermuda) 4th December 1989
[18] James Stockdale comment 6th April 2009
[19] Steamship Mutual (Bermuda) 1st November 1977
[20] *Time* Magazine 26th December 1977
[21] Steamship Mutual (Bermuda) 1st November 1977
[22] Steamship Mutual (Bermuda) 4th December 1989
[23] Steamship Mutual (Bermuda) 8th November 1978

Achille Lauro, passenger vessel

was reported missing about 600 miles off Djibouti, whilst en route from Kohsichang to Italy with a part cargo of molasses. Contact was lost following a final call for assistance on 26th June, when it was reported that the vessel was taking water in No. 1 hold and had requested tug assistance as gale force winds persisted. On 28th June, the owners asked the Club whether an air search for the vessel could be organised at her last reported position. The Club's Djibouti correspondents were contacted and they replied that the French Navy would undertake a search on a payment of $40,000. The Club advised the owners that they could not guarantee the payment of these costs, but the owners nevertheless requested the search to continue. Unfortunately, it was not successful and the vessel was subsequently confirmed lost with all hands. The sum of $39,594 was paid to the French Navy by the owners in September 1985. The Directors agreed unanimously to reimburse the claim. Subsequently, as the result of adverse media attention and comment, the French authorities changed their policy and no longer charged for this humanitarian service.[24]

The incident that made world wide headlines was the case of the hijacking of the *Achille Lauro*, a cruise ship which was owned by and named after one of the longest serving Directors of the Club. The papers described it as 'an act of armed piracy unparalleled in recent Middle East history'. Twelve Palestinian gunmen with reported links to the Palestinian Liberation Organisation (PLO) took 450 passengers hostage off Port Said in October 1985. One American passenger who was confined to a wheelchair was killed. The case was dealt with at the most senior level of the US, Italian and Egyptian Governments, involving the Presidents of all the countries at a time of great delicacy in the Middle East peace process.[25] Although agreed as a war risk, the case remained open for many years. It has the dubious distinction of being the only Club claim to have been made into an opera. *The Death of Klinghoffer* by the American composer, John Adams, was first performed in 1991 and instantly became highly controversial. It was later made into a film.[26]

Claims Management and Unlimited Liability

One ongoing discussion throughout the period was that of limitation of cover. The London Group and then the International Group had always been in favour of unlimited levels of cover, but concerns were being raised over the impact of the enormous and seemingly ever growing size of claims, leading some to suggest that the time had come for a limit on Club cover. By 1986 the Club Boards were divided on the issue: eight Clubs, Steamship Mutual, Newcastle, West of England, North of England, London, Sunderland, Shipowners and Swedish Club were in favour of some form of limit. Against the limit were Britannia, Japan, Skuld, Gard, Liverpool & London, United Kingdom and Standard. In terms of entered tonnage, those opposing limitation represented around 70 per cent of all tonnage entered with the International Group. Steamship had long been in favour of limiting and Sydney Crowe had spoken in favour of it to the London Group as early as 1959.[27] In the event the International Group finally did reach a compromise agreement, spurred on by the imminent 10 year review of the IGA by the EU Commission, and finally made the historic change in 1996.[28]

New Business

1970 to 1987 has been termed the greatest crisis in the shipping industry in the twentieth century as the world share of shipping moved from the traditional maritime nations such as Britain, Greece and Norway to flags of convenience (FOCs) and Asia. By 1987 more than a third of the world fleet was registered in FOCs compared to just 5 per cent in the early 1950s.[29] In 1978 46 per cent of crews on Liberian registered vessels were from South Korea, the Philippines and Taiwan. FOCs were increasingly being used in order to employ low-cost crews.[30] Overall, there was a major decline in the number of vessels flying the flags of the traditional maritime nations resulting from the increased use of FOCs and the growth of the 'tiger' economies of the Far East. However these statistics can be misleading as at least one detailed study has shown that beneficial ownership did not change nearly as much as the flag state.

Inter club competition was increasingly severe, especially in times of recession. Lack of growth in world fleets meant Club tonnage growth could only be achieved by switches between Clubs and, with the number of Scandinavian ships being sold, both the Skuld and the Gard Clubs were seeking tonnage aggressively.[31] During this time, Norway, once the fourth largest register of ships, fell to eighteenth by 1987.[32] From Steamship's perspective growth in membership meant a greater spread of risk and the Directors' support of

[24] Steamship Mutual (Bermuda) 3rd December 1985, James Stockdale 7th April 2009

[25] *The Times* 8th–12th October 1985

[26] http://www.channel4.com/culture/microsites/K/ the_death_of_klinghoffer/

[27] Steamship Mutual (Bermuda) 11th November 1959

[28] Steamship Mutual (Bermuda) 8th December 1986

[29] Stig Tenold, 'Exodus Explained – The Fate of Ships sold from Norway, 1970–1987', *Mariner's Mirror*, Vol. 92, No. 3, (August 2006), 300–308, p. 301

[30] Tenold, 'Exodus Explained', p. 305

[31] Steamship Mutual (Bermuda) 20th March 1979

[32] Tenold, 'Exodus Explained', p. 301

Seminar in Korea with Jim Howard-Smith, Joe Hughes and James Stockdale from Steamship

Manila seminar 1979, with James Stockdale, Jim Howard-Smith and Joe Hughes from Steamship

expansion resulted in new countries being targeted. In 1978 a long term Director, Sandy Struthers, suggested South America and the Managers were soon visiting Argentina, Chile and Peru.

Increasing the Club's tonnage meant the Managers travelling actively to all parts of the globe and they were supported by introductions from the Directors. Together with active travel, advertising became an important part of the Club's budget and new methods of raising the profile of the Club were under consideration. In 1978 the advertising budget was more than £13,000 spread over six regular shipping periodicals. In general, the format used was a standard brand image to keep the Club's name in front of readers. Space was also obtained periodically for special articles in publications such as *Lloyd's List P&I* editions. Around this time, the Club brought out a new publication, a newsletter for members called *Sea Venture,* and since its first publication *Lloyd's List* and others have used many extracts and given the Club due credit for them. Realising the value of this, advertising material was co-ordinated with the production of *Sea Venture* with the major emphasis on the service delivered by the Club.[33] Seminars became another way of raising the Club's profile. Papers were delivered on a variety of topics, to invited audiences and the seminars were held in various parts of the world. The seminars were seen as a valuable addition, both assisting in loss prevention and enhancing the reputation of the Club for expertise and service. While the original intention had been to hold the seminars in markets new to P&I, rather than in sophisticated markets such as Germany, Italy and India, it soon emerged that they were also useful in disseminating information on new developments of a legal or technical nature. In 1980, the Managers reported that the Club had taken a stand at the Expoship Sea Trade Exhibition in Hong Kong, as well as at Posidonia in Piraeus, attracting large numbers of visitors with the resultant publicity.[34]

The active promotion of the Club in these various ways, through print, seminars and visits began to show dividends and by February 1980 there was a total of 25,216,104 tons entered. This comprised both increased size and number of vessels from existing members as well as new entries. By now the 6 million tons entered from Hong Kong had overtaken the Italian tonnage as the largest regional entry and represented 24 per cent of the entered tonnage. Credit for this was given to the 'additional canvassing by the younger Managers travelling abroad and, the Managers believed, by making every effort to give the best possible service to members'.[35] The increase in entered tonnage of 20 per cent against an increase in world tonnage of 2.3 per cent suggests that the increase was gained primarily from other Clubs rather than new buildings.

In 1983 the Oceanus Club, an independent mutual which was not part of the International Group, was in difficulties and this led to the Club receiving a high number of additional enquiries. Oceanus had been in existence since the 1960s and had been successful in acquiring tonnage in the short term, particularly from the national state fleets which were required to tender for the lowest bid, through its aggressive policy of undercutting rates. The most immediate cause of Oceanus' problems was allegations of serious non-disclosure that resulted in their failure to make recoveries from their French reinsurers, and led to it ceasing underwriting new business with effect from 20th February 1984. The increased number of enquiries to Steamship as a result of this was not necessarily all good news as Steamship declined to quote on the majority of the business as it was 'not of a type that would have been of advantage to the Club'.[36] Nevertheless some quality business did come from that source, including the return of the Pakistan National Shipping Corporation and the Shipping Corporation of India Limited, both still represented on the Club Board 25 years later.

One side effect of the failure of the Oceanus Club and its consequent inability to honour its guarantees, was the questioning of the acceptability of some Clubs' letters of undertaking. Once trust is lost, questions are naturally asked of other similar organisations. Consideration had to be given to providing more bank guarantees in the

The first edition of
Steamship's newsletter,
Sea Venture, in 1978

Cosco Pacific,
the Cosco Container Line Co Ltd,
China

[33] Steamship Mutual (Bermuda) 28th November 1978   [35] Steamship Mutual (Bermuda) 18th March 1980
[34] Steamship Mutual (Bermuda) 22nd September 1980   [36] Steamship Mutual (Bermuda) 15th March 1983

short term and a joint Group circular was issued to confirm the continued viability of the International Group and of its reinsurance arrangements.[37]

One area of new business was to cause considerable debate within the International Group.

> By the early 1980's it was clear that China was an emerging economic power. The Club wished to participate in the growing Chinese shipping market. Some Clubs were already insuring Chinese fleets. However, there was a desire within China to develop the insurance business on a co-operative basis; 'technology transfer' were the buzzwords of the time. The Club's Managers believed that this was an entirely reasonable wish and entered into negotiations with brokers in Hong Kong and counterparties in China to explore an acceptable method of co-operation. As a result of these discussions the Club obtained an entry of 88 vessels, approximately 800,000 grt from owners in China. These vessels were all entered in the China Protection & Indemnity Club but with a direct entry into Steamship Mutual in respect of claims in excess of a deductible of US$400,000. Much to the Managers' surprise, the arrangement was to prove to be hugely controversial. Some Members of the International Group suggested that the arrangement was tantamount to a reinsurance of the China Protection & Indemnity Club and consequently a breach of an International Group Agreement. Many months of difficult discussions within the International Group followed. Throughout this time the Board stood firmly behind the Managers believing that the stance taken was not only correct in law and fully compliant with the International Group Agreement, but was also in the best long term interests of both shipowners in China and the International Group as a whole. The Club has always believed that free and open competition within markets is vital to shipowners and their P&I Clubs. Fortunately the matter was finally resolved with an acceptance that the Club was not in breach of the International Group Agreement. Many International Group Clubs now operate in China in exactly the same way as Steamship Mutual.[38]

Later, another new market opened up with the collapse of communism in Eastern Europe, exemplified by the fall of the Berlin Wall in 1989. Now the former Soviet Union countries and their allies who were in need of P&I began to look outside the confines of the local state controlled domestic insurance companies to the International Group Clubs in search of better service and more flexible terms.

People Changes

It is inevitable in any organisation that tragedy will impact at some stage and two major figures were lost at relatively young ages. Peter Dorey was the head of Onesimus Dorey Shipowners of Guernsey and was a Conseiller (a member of the Guernsey parliament), becoming one of their leading statesmen. He had been a director since 1955 and was lost in the Fastnet race in 1979 at the age of 51. This race is an endurance race for ocean going yachts and is considered highly challenging. That year a freak storm blew up in the

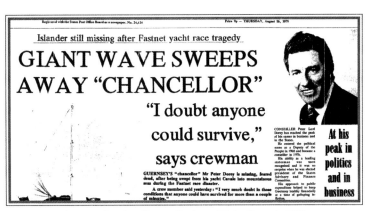

Guernsey Post headline on the loss of Peter Dorey in 1979

Irish Sea and claimed the lives of fifteen people. Dorey, a very experienced yachtsman, was swept from his yacht *Cavale* by a huge wave and his body was never found.[39] It was ironic for such a supporter of P&I that one of the good things to come out of the tragedy was that it became mandatory for all yachts to carry VHS radios, many did not in 1979 and consequently were unable to report their position to the emergency services as they drifted in high seas. As further precautions, the number of yachts allowed to enter the subsequent Fastnet races was restricted to 300 and qualifications for competing were introduced.

Dorey had been an active member of the Committee and the Board, and took a particularly keen interest in the investment strategy. Another of his concerns was the Club's image and he suggested that the name Steamship Mutual was more associated with the nineteenth century (apparently not realising it had been chosen in the early twentieth century). His proposal was to change it to 'Worldship Mutual'. Howard Morgan's response was that in the 'insurance world old names breed confidence and new ones are often suspect' and he pointed out the number of other Clubs that had 'Steam Ship' in their names. The suggestion was never taken up.[40]

There was a major structural change within the Managers, Alfred Stocken and Company. It had been a limited company and this had been changed to a proprietary partnership in 1965 with the introduction of corporation tax. The majority of the equity was held by Sydney Crowe and his family and his formal retirement gave rise to the need to make further structural changes and bring in a non-capital structure to facilitate generational change for the benefit of future partners. This meant effectively negotiating a management buyout. With the support of the Board, a gentlemanly and amicable arrangement was reached. For the continuing Managers a new Management Agreement with the Club was drawn up and approved. The Agreement was simple and

[37] Steamship Mutual (Bermuda) 20th March 1984
[38] Gary Rynsard, 21st May 2009
[39] *Guernsey Evening Press* 16th August 1979
[40] Correspondence Peter Dorey/Howard Morgan 2nd February 1973

straightforward stating, amongst other things, that only active Managers were to be admitted to the management.[41] This was the final split from the past and reflects the change from a traditional paternalistic organisation, which was quite common in Crowe's day, to a more modern partnership. A further sign of the maturing organisation followed this change. In the past the recruitment policy was to recruit 'associate managers' of the Club with the open intention that they would become full managers after a period of time. In the previously small organisation this had worked well, but the growth of the business called for new career paths to create a middle management group.[42]

The Young Team

The other major change was the reorganisation of the London office. Howard Morgan had partially retired in 1982 when he had moved to Bermuda and handed over the running of the London office to Alan Tolhurst. He returned to London in 1984 and briefly resumed the active position as Senior Partner until his final retirement in 1985.

> *Howard Morgan was born in 1921 in Cardiff. He was educated in Somerset where he won prizes for rifle shooting. During the war he was in the Army including service in North Africa, Normandy, Italy and Burma and gained the rank of Captain. After discharge he joined Middle Temple Inn of Court and commenced to read for the Bar but joined Steamship Mutual before sitting the final exams. Following his retirement he became a name at Lloyd's. His shrewd judgement and knowledge of the insurance industry enabled him to make a success of this even though Lloyd's was undergoing some of the most difficult years in its history. He died in December 2000.*[43]

His son recalls that he displayed sound judgement in everything he did and he had a great sense of humour. From the Club's perspective his leadership during the currency crisis and the move to Bermuda were some of his many significant contributions to the Club.

Alan Tolhurst, who had been acting Senior Partner while Howard Morgan was in Bermuda, finally took over. An ambitious man, a lawyer by training, who had for many years been in charge of claims, he had been determined to make significant changes to the management.

> *Even before taking over from Howard Morgan, AT decided to try and establish a coherent succession plan for the management of the business by recruiting a series of young lawyers, starting with David Staines in 1967, conscious that his then partners were ageing and would need to be supplemented/replaced over time by new young professionals. His soon to be successor, George Greenwood followed in 1977, hotly followed by James Stockdale and Gary Rynsard in 1978.*[44]

Alan Tolhurst's ambitions were cut short by his premature death from cancer at the age of 56. He had made a big impact in his career and was a somewhat controversial personality. 'A taskmaster, but above all else he was always fair' is one description and in his funeral eulogy he was described as an 'ebullient, witty and strong willed, forceful personality' with an 'enormous range of knowledge'.[45] John Lean, a Director, recalls:

Alan Tolhurst was then the Senior Partner of Alfred Stocken, and we very quickly established a very robust friendship, which included a regular dinner with himself and his family, along with specially invited managers. Alan was a very outspoken individual, and the Club was then run on very 'old traditional', almost Master and Servant, lines. The partners were all ensconced on the top floor of the old Aquatical House building on Bishopsgate, and it was quite rare to sight any of the senior partners on any of the 'working floors'. Alan took pride in progressively replacing the 'Old Guard' of partners, such as the Howard-Smiths, the Crowes and Howard Morgan with a relatively young and dynamic team.[46]

After Alan's death these young men, including Gary Rynsard, became the new face of Steamship. 1986 also saw the death of Sydney Crowe at the age of 80. Howard Morgan read the funeral address and was eloquent in his praise for the man who had brought the Club into the international field.

The new senior partner was George Greenwood who had only become a partner in 1980. The management team of Steamship was conscious that they were now the youngest team among the P&I clubs, George was 37 and the rest were mainly in their 30s, and they set out to show what they could do.[47] In George Greenwood's words 'we

Alan Tolhurst visiting the
Oranjeland wreck in 1973

[41] Steamship Mutual (Bermuda) 20th October 1981
[42] Steamship Mutual (Bermuda) 9th July 1985
[43] Julian Morgan correspondence 2009
[44] James Stockdale April 2009

[45] Letter Margaret Webb to H Doe 2nd May 2009;
    Funeral Eulogy by Nicholas Healy Jr.
[46] John Lean email to H Doe 18th January 2009
[47] Interview George Greenwood 6th November 2008

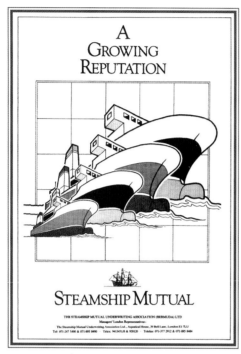

A
GROWING
REPUTATION

STEAMSHIP MUTUAL

THE STEAMSHIP MUTUAL UNDERWRITING ASSOCIATION (BERMUDA) LTD
Managers' London Representatives:
The Steamship Mutual Underwriting Association Ltd., Aquatical House, 39 Bell Lane, London E1 7LU
Tel: 071-247 5490 & 071-895 8490 · Telex: 941345/8 & 928120 · Telefax: 071-377 2912 & 071-895 8484

Steamship advertisement

George Greenwood, senior partner
on the cover of *Fairplay*

were conscious of being the new boys on the block. We saw ourselves as having more enthusiasm, hungrier for business, more internationally minded and more prepared to go the extra mile'.[48] In 1987 the Directors were presented with a marketing strategy for the Club and this would from now on become a regular feature each year. They targeted the insurance managers of shipping companies and travelled the world to see them. In 1990, George recalled a chance encounter at Brazil airport with Roger Elliott who was then chairman of Willis Faber the insurance giant. Willis Faber had offices in almost every country but Elliott had never previously visited South America, a continent with which by then, George and his fellow partners were very familiar.

The activity began to pay off as early as 1987 with tonnage increasing by a record 3.3 million grt to nearly 32 million grt. Much of this was due to the decision of the Shipowners' P&I Club to withdraw the major part of its reinsurance contract from the West of England Club, with whom it had been placed since the 1950s, and to place the programme with Steamship Mutual. That placement was responsible for an increase in the entered tonnage of 2.56 million grt. Additionally the Chairman, Sandy Struthers, put on record the assistance given to the Managers in 'promoting the Association in many parts of the world during the year'.[49]

In a climate of escalating claims and lower investment income there was, at this time, a considerable shifting of tonnage between Clubs. Claims were accelerating at an unprecedented rate, and had arrived in an era of historically low premiums, which would no longer be buttressed by as favourable an investment climate. There were major movements in 1989 of tonnage out of the London Club, the West of England and even from Standard, while tonnage was moving to Steamship, Gard and Britannia. Steamship's marketing strategy was to concentrate its efforts on continually improving service to existing members and 'thereby maintain the presently high reputation of the Association' combined with carefully planned and strategic marketing. Markets where the Club was traditionally represented and where the Managers would be actively promoting the Club with potential new entries were Italy, India, Hong Kong, Korea and Canada. Other markets where the Club was not well established and where their presence would contribute to the Club's spread of risk and stability were Spain, France, Netherlands and Scandinavia. In the United States and some parts of South America, a more cautious approach was to be taken.[50]

Subsidiaries

George Greenwood saw the importance of subsidiaries and their establishment in Brazil and Hong Kong came about, but for very different reasons. From 1968 the Club had an exclusive representation agreement with Dr. Horacio Milliet, the principal of Lloyd Paulista in Brazil. It had been highly successful and Noel Howard-Smith, the Steamship Manager responsible, suggested that Martin Hubbard, a member of Steamship's staff then working on the Brazilian business, should move to Rio de Janeiro to work in the Lloyd Paulista office in 1981. Unfortunately Dr Milliet became ill and there was no natural successor with similar abilities in his organisation. The logical step was to establish a local Steamship office under Hubbard's management and this was set up in 1984. Perhaps, not surprisingly, Lloyd Paulista, still owned by the Milliet family, were less convinced of the need for this and a dispute arose over loss of commission when their contract was brought to an end. A financial settlement was finally agreed with the Board's approval in 1986.[51]

Significant entries were built up, not only from China, including Hong Kong and Taiwan, but also from Korea, the Philippines, Thailand, Australia and Singapore and by 1987 the Far East represented 25 per cent of the Club's tonnage. With those economies expanding fast, the tonnage from the region could only continue to grow. However, looking after the members there was made more difficult by the travel distances, time zones and cost. Fewer visits would mean that the Managers were less well informed about some of these markets on a day to day basis than they would ideally wish to be. Other Clubs were already establishing a local presence and it was now felt that the time was right to open an office in Hong Kong. The Managers had secured the services of a Hong Kong Chinese resident, Mr Edward Lee, who had many years' experience working both on the shipowning and broking sides of the industry. They also had available, on an extremely competitive basis,

48 Interview George Greenwood 12th February 2009
49 Steamship Mutual (Bermuda) 17th March 1987
50 Steamship Mutual (Bermuda) 17th March 1987
51 Steamship Mutual (Bermuda) 1st July 1986;
   George Greenwood 1st July 2009

premises on Hong Kong Island which belonged to Pioneer Insurance Company Limited of the Philippines, a company with which the Club had collaborated in relation to Philippine business for very many years. It was envisaged that the office would provide a liaison point for the Managers in relation to all Far Eastern business, whether produced by brokers or entered directly with the Club. Both the offices in Brazil and Hong Kong continue to provide valuable services to the Club and its members.[52]

New Types of Business

Expansion of the Club into other types of business was also under discussion. David Clarabut was a Director but was also the Chairman of Shipowners Club (SOP). The two Clubs came together in a joint venture, the insurance of charterers' liabilities. For many years, this had been undertaken by owners' P&I Clubs, although the requirements of owners and charterers differed from one another in two important respects. The first of these was that charterers' cover was subject to a limit of liability and the second was that the cover was predominately underwritten on a fixed premium, rather than on a mutual basis. In 1986 roughly $4.5 million of charterers' P&I cover was underwritten by Steamship, of which approximately $3.75 million was 'owner associated'. The remainder was 'pure charterer' i.e. not associated with an owned entry. The view was that the business could be expanded and in some Clubs as much as 20 per cent of their total entry consisted of charterer members.[53] James Stockdale recalls that

> In order to differentiate Steamship in this area of business, it was decided to set up an independent reinsurance Trust in Bermuda, along the lines of the Steamship Mutual Trust, called, imaginatively, the Charterers Mutual Insurance Trust, to provide a dedicated reinsurance arrangement for 'pure' charterers, reinsured in its turn totally outside the Group system through the Lloyd's market. This was designed to protect the Club from exposure to any large charterers' losses and avoid any perceived conflict of interest between the owners' and charterers' sides of the business.[54]

Oil rigs were viewed as another potential area for business expansion, but opinion was divided. Steamship had previously insured navigating rigs from time to time, but non navigating rigs were excluded from the Pooling Agreement. The Scandinavian Clubs had established a separate market and were able to quote advantageous terms, backed by non-Group reinsurance. Initially, the decision was that it was better for Steamship to remain with those areas within which they specialised.[55]

Technology

When Doreen McDonnell joined Steamship in 1951 as a shorthand typist the Club circulars were produced on a Gestetner machine and paper was still in short supply. Howard Morgan joined on the same day and he recalled that his

> … first job was that of Assistant Underwriter i.e. assistant to Jim Howard-Smith. Those were the days before electronic calculators and premium calculations could be rather long winded. The calculation involved a separate entrance fee and the proportionate part of the year for each of three classes. On my first day, just before I left for luncheon, Jim passed to me for arithmetical checking six cases which he had worked on during the morning. After luncheon I confirmed the calculations within minutes – which clearly surprised Jim. He did not know that during a short pre-war period with Royal Insurance I had been introduced to the assistant underwriter's indispensable companion – a book of some 50 pages of closely printed calculations entitled Odd Timetables, and I had managed to buy a copy during the luncheon period. I was able to conceal the book for about seven days but then confessed that I was not entirely unaided. Some months later I was transferred to the Claims Department and I donated Odd Timetables to my successor.[56]

When Larry Cork joined the accounts department of Steamship in 1959 all calculations were done by hand. Even 15 years later when Peter Hicks joined as an underwriter

C J Ahrenkiel, Ahrenkiel Consulting Services, Berne
Committee member and former Chairman

[52] George Greenwood, James Stockdale comments July 2009
[53] Steamship Mutual (Bermuda) 17th March 1986
[54] James Stockdale 7th April 2009
[55] Steamship Mutual (Bermuda) 3rd April 1989
[56] Morgan, SSM History draft

much was still done manually although the accounts department did by then have a computer. Instalments were manually typed up and complex calculations were done by the comptometer operator. In 1975 came a major change when each underwriter was given their own calculator together with one hour of training.[57] But by the 1980s it was a question not just of one computer but a computer system of personal computers and specially designed software. The volume of data that had to be collected and collated was substantial with approximately 5,000 new claims files opened each year, some of which included more than 40 sub-claims.[58] Such was the nature of change and the growing complexity of the business that by 2005 all network requirements were outsourced.

New Office

As the business grew, yet again finding space for both staff and computers in central London remained a challenge, particularly as the area of Bishopsgate in which the London office was situated was earmarked by British Rail for redevelopment (this is now Broadgate) and so the fourth move of Steamship came about.

By 1984 Steamship Mutual Bermuda had grown to 30 million grt and the Bermuda Managers were still using Steamship Mutual London as London Representatives. In a few years the Broadgate development scheme emerged and towards the end of the decade the developers needed to demolish the Bishopsgate building and paid

The current Aquatical House, artist's impression

£9 million to acquire it. After a year in temporary accommodation in Mark Lane, the staff of Steamship Mutual London moved to a larger building in Bell Lane. The Bermuda Club tonnage continued to expand and at 20th February 1995 the 'mutual' tonnage stood at approximately 45 million grt from about 35 different countries.[59]

Regulatory Authorities

The International Group Clubs were still under the scrutiny of the British Government and in 1987 a high court judgement resulted in the Department of Trade and Industry approaching the Bermuda based clubs requiring them to be licensed under the 1978 Insurance Companies Act.

After protracted negotiations, the three Bermuda based Clubs finally agreed to apply under protest, a step which was later to have the then unforeseen tax consequences referred to previously. Somewhat ironically considering that Steamship was already a licensed insurer in an EU state, the next structural change was the establishment of a European based subsidiary Club. Although, up until then, P&I had not been affected by the EU Non Life Establishment Directives, concern was growing that one or more EU states could implement legislation requiring vessels registered in that country to place their P&I insurance with an insurer 'established' within the EU. In order to pre-empt that risk, in 1995 Steamship Mutual Underwriting Association (Europe) Ltd was incorporated in Luxembourg, as a subsidiary of Steamship Mutual (Bermuda) and 95 per cent reinsured by Bermuda thus enabling Steamship to obtain the necessary financial services passport in Europe.[60]

In 1996 the International Group began its application for extension of its exemption from Article 81 of the Treaty of Rome. George Greenwood, Steamship's senior partner, was by now chairman of the International Group and so became very involved with the European Union debate. There was, at the time, a group of both brokers and some shipowners who, with the aid of the press, used the opportunity to make a concerted attack on the IG, as they had in 1985. The concerns over the application caused many of the Clubs to re-examine their corporate structure and business models. As a result there was a move by some Clubs towards diversification and/or consolidation. The Liverpool & London and Newcastle Clubs were absorbed by North of England, while the Standard, UK and Britannia diversified into other types of mutual insurance. The Steamship Managers considered the pros and cons of alternative structures including the possibility of cross-selling multiple marine insurance lines to their shipowner members. The various arguments were put to the Directors of Steamship, who, after considerable debate, rejected all the various suggestions in favour of remaining a pure monoline P&I insurer. Attention was then switched to diversification within P&I and the previously explored rig

[57] Larry Cork, Doreen McDonnell, Peter Hicks, December 2008
[58] Steamship Mutual (Bermuda) 9th July 1985
[59] Morgan, SSM History draft
[60] James Stockdale 7th April 2009

insurance became a reality. With plenty of experience handling personal injury claims, it seemed a good fit and was set up on a fixed premium basis. It was not in the event an entirely successful business and was dogged by reinsurance problems both in Lloyd's and the North American markets. The business was placed in run-off in 2000 although the Managers continued to be involved in the provision of claims and underwriting services to the Bermuda based mutual energy underwriter Aegis and their Lloyd's managing agency, to whom some of the book had been transferred.[61]

Meanwhile the EU debate continued and George, with the strong support of the majority of shipowners, led the IG in helping the EU Commission to understand once more the very different business model the Clubs represented. It was felt that some concessions might need to be found for the EU who had not fully realised the commercial importance and strength of the shipping industry. The Group now insured 90 per cent of world shipping. The Group had been slow to understand the importance of the lobbying process in Brussels but now it finally mobilised its resources in earnest and shipowners from around the world made their points forcefully to the European Commission. In the end, with some minor adjustments, the agreement was extended for another ten years from 1999.[62] John Lean was chairman of Steamship at the time and remembers the EU Commission debates well. There was also a view at the time that further changes within the EU might give preference to locally registered insurers and it was therefore deemed prudent to establish Steamship Mutual (Europe) in Luxembourg in February 1994 and it commenced underwriting in February 1995.[63]

CC Tung, Orient Overseas (International) Ltd, Hong Kong Committee member and former Chairman

Isabella Grimaldi, Grimaldi Holdings SPA and first lady board member 1999

Major Claims

The collision of the freight ferry *Adige* and a passenger vessel, *Jupiter* in Piraeus harbour in 1983 became a significant case for two reasons. The *Jupiter*, with 400 English schoolchildren on board for an educational cruise, had its side ripped open and sank quickly. There were four fatalities but the potential for disaster could have been much greater. The master of the *Adige* was detained in Greece for 53 days and this was an early example of what has become an increasing trend for direct action to be taken against a ship's master in the wake of serious casualties. A very large security demand was made by the Greek owners of the *Jupiter* and rather than provide a guarantee for this amount the ship was left in situ while negotiations progressed. The issue of liability was resolved within three months but the personal injury claims took years to resolve as the impact of post traumatic stress was only in the early stages of being recognised by the English legal system.

In 1993 one of the biggest claims came from one of the Club's smallest vessels. The *Mauvilla* was a push tug operating on the Alabama River. It was pushing a convoy of six barges two abreast and had left Mobile in the early hours of the morning in thick fog. In the fog the barge entered a tributary of the river by mistake and encountered a railway bridge, displacing the centre span by a few inches. Just minutes later an Amtrak express passenger train was derailed and locomotives and carriages fell into the river destroying the bridge in the process. The loss of life was tragically high, 49 people lost their lives and 175 were injured. Understandably there was considerable press coverage with lurid if incorrect tales concerning the 'alligator infested bayou'.[64]

Hanjin Pennsylvania suffered a serious explosion and fire originating in her containerised cargo in November 2002

Removal of the last of the wreckage of the *Nedlloyd Recife* at São Francisco do Sul, Brazil following her grounding in 1996

[61] Interview George Greenwood 12th February 2009; James Stockdale April 2009

[62] Interview George Greenwood 12th February 2009

[63] John Lean, George Greenwood, James Stockdale comments July 2009

[64] *Fairplay* 15th July 1994

Container ships are now well established but their very structure and size can bring different problems as in the case of the *Nedlloyd Recife*. This was a 1,600 TEU vessel that ran aground in Brazil in 1997. Chris Adams of Steamship recalls it well:

> *The wreck removal was extremely expensive due to the problems of the local geography. The ship ran aground on a small island and could not be reached from the seaward side due to the ocean swell. From the landward side access was much easier because the wreck was effectively acting as a breakwater blocking the entrance to a small bay. However landward access involved the construction of a road across the island and docks at either end of it, and their removal on completion of the operation, all of which formed part of the claim. Additionally, as the vessel was a cellular containership, its list made it difficult to unload the containers. Over time, all the holds became tidal, containers disintegrated with a dangerous mixture of chemicals, which had to be contained and removed in a controlled manner.[65]*

The bill came to $60 million, a total now exceeded multiple times by the MSC *Napoli* (not insured by Steamship but by the London P&I Club), which was grounded off the coast of Devon in January 2007.[66]

The Ship Safety Trust

Loss prevention has become an ever more important task for the Club. In common with most other clubs, it was decided in the 1990s to increase the scope and frequency of ship inspections and a condition survey department was set up to consider the safety of the ships including the qualification and training of crews. Crew experience has changed, with many mixed nationality crews, few of whom have any sense of corporate identity and may just work a single voyage for a company. The Ship Safety Trust was set up during George Greenwood's time as senior partner. Funded by the Managers, it develops training materials for use on board ship, such as CDs, DVDs and posters, with all royalties going back into the Trust to fund further projects.

One of the DVDs produced was in response to the *Erika* disaster when the oil tanker of that name sank in the Bay of Biscay in 1999. 20,000 tons of oil were lost, coating about 250 miles of French coastline in one of the most environmentally sensitive areas. Lessons had been learned about clearing up oil and, according to *The Times* report in 2002:

> *However, there is a positive story to emerge from Brittany's experience. Looking at the coastline today there is absolutely no evidence of the disaster. The clean-up operation has been so thorough that the coast's micro-ecology has been restored to almost normal. This coast that ends at the point where the Loire meets the Atlantic is among the most exclusive in France and Europe because of the spas, hotels and beaches. Yet tourism is now back to pre-1999 levels, having dipped by a relatively modest amount of 20 per cent in 2000.[67]*

The loss of the *Erika* in 1999

Ipswich Trader at Charlestown in the 1930s

The *Cosco Busan*, a 5,500 TEU container vessel, became the cause of the largest ever claim on the Club when, with a pilot on board, it hit the San Francisco-Oakland Bay Bridge in November 2007 and discharged more than 53,000 gallons of bunker oil into San Francisco Bay. The incident was reported widely in the press and the claim, like so many, is complex and still ongoing.[68]

Claims over time have changed in both scale and complexity and it is worth making a comparison with the early years of Steamship Mutual. John Raddings was the master of the *Ipswich Trader*, a 397 ton coastal steamship operating in the 1930s. This was owned by Horlock's of Mistley one of the Club's earliest Committee members. Raddings, who later became a very experienced Humber pilot, had a perspective on arriving at a dock which is a useful reminder for those who only know

> ...*jetties that are made from steel, concrete and rubber. As jetties were wooden, landing a vessel meant the jetty would generally, creek, screech, sing, or groan as the timbers took the strain. However, if a ship landed over enthusiastically the top deck planking or walkway would ripple like the keys on a piano and if lucky, the ship would be gently repelled in the direction from whence it came. In the event of any impact damage wooden jetties are very kind to ships, which generally is taken up solely by the wood. The ship just reverses away, complete with embarrassed red faces all around. After a quick check up and a bit of luck, ship and maybe relieved captain, just sail away.*[69]

In the early years claims were small, quickly settled and environmental issues simply did not arise. Attitudes have changed, as have the size of ships together with increased media and political attention, and not always for the better.

[65] Chris Adams June 2009
[66] Chris Adams interview 6th November 2008
[67] *The Times* 20th November 2002
[68] *Lloyd's List* 20th February 2009
[69] David Raddings, 'Memories of John Raddings, 1910 to 2000', unpublished notes

Steamship in the Twenty-First Century

Steamship entered the twenty-first century in good shape. Its expansion had continued and from 1985 to 1998 its percentage share of the contributing tonnage in the International Group had grown from 8 per cent to 11 per cent (see Table opposite) with Steamship Bermuda obtaining an AM Best interactive 'A' rating.

In December 1999 the Boards of the two Clubs announced a major reorganisation. The absence of an agreement with the Luxembourg Commissariat over gross reserving and the localisation of reserves had resulted in Steamship Europe ceasing underwriting at 20th February 1999 and going into run-off. To meet the need for a European established underwriter it was decided to reactivate Steamship London.

In the event a 'reorganisation sub committee' was established, consisting of present and past chairmen, to consider the pros and cons of totally reorganising the Club structure to allow Steamship London to re-apply for a UK License to resume insurance activities. Since 1979, following the formation of Steamship Bermuda in 1975, Steamship London had fulfilled two functions – running off its own business and acting as the London Representative of the Bermuda Managers under the direction of the partners of Alfred Stocken.

The reorganisation thus entailed the re-naming of Alfred Stocken as Steamship Insurance Management (SIM) and the termination of Steamship London's activities as the Managers' London Representative and employer of the London based staff. In its place Steamship Insurance Management Services Limited (SIMSL) was set up as a wholly owned subsidiary of SIM. Relieved of its representative function, Steamship London was then free to apply for a licence to recommence underwriting. This should have been a relatively straightforward procedure but, as the consequence of unfortunate timing, the application ran into complications following the creation of the Financial Services Authority (FSA) and the transfer of the Department of Trade's insurance supervisory functions. Because of these delays Steamship London was not finally able to start underwriting again until 20th February 2003.[70]

In 2001 Steamship London applied to the Department of Trade and Industry (DTI) for a licence to underwrite just as the fevered 'dotcom' bubble burst and the equity markets began to collapse. In November the FSA took over the supervision of insurance from the DTI. The FSA took a stricter view than its predecessor of corporate governance, directors' responsibilities and risk and so Steamship London had to re-present its application to underwrite under the new FSA rules and was eventually granted its licence in November 2002. Corporate governance had become high profile and attitudes were changing. Gone were the days when 'leading merchant banks' could express astonishment at being barred from dealing in the shares of companies they were advising during takeover battles.[71] This conflict of interest may be obvious today, but was simply not considered in 1985.

Table 2: Changes in the International Group Contributing Tonnage,
courtesy of the International Group

	1985 Tonnage	% Contribution	1998 Tonnage	% Contribution
American	0	0%	5,168,147	1%
Britannia	56,495,373	16%	58,123,011	12%
Gard	26,852,216	7%	53,790,902	11%
Japan	0	0%	41,824,741	9%
Liverpool & London	3,942,063	1%	6,475,920	1%
London	30,122,043	8%	25,332,040	5%
Newcastle	3,108,028	1%	0	0%
North of England	3,547,532	1%	21,784,113	5%
Shipowners	0	0%	0	0%
Skuld	21,454,993	6%	39,294,651	8%
Standard	27,729,056	8%	31,168,096	7%
Steamship Mutual	27,721,826	8%	51,913,075	11%
Sunderland	2,608,045	1%	0	0%
Swedish	4,227,977	1%	11,689,476	2%
United Kingdom	107,524,414	30%	86,809,848	18%
West of England	45,426,373	13%	36,913,740	8%

Meanwhile the equity market collapse following the terrorist attack on the Twin Towers in New York (9/11) had adversely affected investments for the Club and, in December 2001, SSMB announced additional calls on the 1999, 2000 and 2001 policy years in order to raise new capital of $114 million. Three factors had combined to force the calls. The rig business was severely exposed due to the bankruptcy of a US reinsurer, Reliance, one of the Club's investment advisors had seriously underperformed and had added to the problems caused by the meltdown in the equity market. On top of all of this was the scrutiny from the FSA who had difficulty in seeing the Club as any different from a commercial insurance organisation and had less faith in the strength and security of the mutual system than their predecessors at the DTI. [72]

> At this time Corporate Governance became a very real issue and for the first time an Audit Committee was formed, comprising myself as Chair, with other members being Otto Fritzner and Herbert Juniel. We had hardly settled into the role when the Club came under the scrutiny of the Financial Services Authority (FSA). Fortunately, almost immediately afterward the financial markets improved to the extent that our investment returns for the year came in at US$75 million – and got us out of immediate trouble, although the regular meetings between the FSA and Audit Committee continued for a couple of years after.[73]

[70] James Stockdale, May 2009; John Lean email to H Doe 18th January 2009
[71] The Times 10th October 1985
[72] James Stockdale, George Greenwood, July 2009
[73] John Lean email to H Doe 2009

Mohammed Souri, National Iranian
Tanker Co., Tehran and Chairman of
Steamship Mutual London

Otto Fritzner, Chairman of Steamship
Mutual Bermuda

The Managers took on the task of an in depth restructuring of the business. A cleansing of the underwriting book resulted in a 25 per cent reduction in entered tonnage and this was accompanied by significant staff redundancies. In 2003 George Greenwood retired after 17 years as senior partner and James Stockdale took his place. The changes continued with a re-evaluation of every aspect of the operation, which resulted, amongst other things, in the internal reorganisation into Syndicates on the basis of geographic responsibilities and a culture of continuous improvement. In line with the times, increasing emphasis was placed on corporate governance, risk management and capital management. Each new senior partner brings his own management style and John Lean observed James' emphasis on transparency between the Managers and the Directors. The organisation into Syndicates meant that the

> ...partners responsible for each Syndicate are located on the same floor as their responsibility. The formation of SIMSL has allowed room for growth and development of senior (and indeed junior) Managers in a chosen career path.'

> Our computer systems have kept pace with the times and technology since the mid 90's and are now at the cutting edge of corporate storage and reporting – a vast difference to the 'button up boots' systems of the earlier decades.

> The strengthening of our Finance and Actuarial sections under the guidance of Steve Ward has made a tremendous impact on Club management and the production of a Business Plan and the subsequent reporting to that Plan leave no doubt as to how the Club is travelling. The Board composition has also markedly changed over the years since my initial appointment. It is now considerably larger – 26 against 19 in 1990, and with a much broader scope of representation. It now has at least seven directors from the Far East, excluding India. The re-structure of the Board into Committees, instituted by Fritzner and Stockdale means that every Director has the opportunity to discuss in depth, matters of concern, rather than feeling constrained by time limitations at the main Board meeting.[74]

The Club has seen many changes in the type of vessels entered and the countries in which these vessels are owned. Detailed comparison is possible from 1975 and the charts make an interesting contrast with 1909 and even with the Club's international expansion in 1950. The charts show the rise and fall in tonnage and the growth of Members in such sectors as the cruise industry.

The hard work and a 'prudent and disciplined' underwriting policy of the last few years has paid off and in May 2008 Steamship was able to report an overall operating surplus of $28 million, up from $800,000 in 2006/07 and an increase in entered tonnage of 9 per cent[75] of group tonnage. The positive contribution of Otto Fritzner, the current Chairman appointed in 2001, in working with his Board Directors and the Managers was recognised when his term was further extended to cover the centenary year.

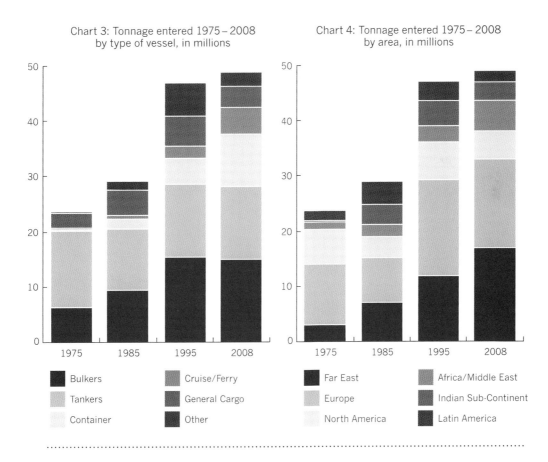

Chart 3: Tonnage entered 1975 – 2008 by type of vessel, in millions

Chart 4: Tonnage entered 1975 – 2008 by area, in millions

Bulkers — Cruise/Ferry — Tankers — General Cargo — Container — Other

Far East — Africa/Middle East — Europe — Indian Sub-Continent — North America — Latin America

[74] John Lean email to H Doe 2009
[75] *Lloyd's List* 19th May 2008

Summary

In 2009 Steamship can look back and see that it has come a very long way from its origins as a small West Country oriented Club specialising in coastal sail to becoming one of the top Clubs in the world. Its success was achieved in an environment where many other Clubs failed as several of the 1909 P&I Clubs no longer exist. In the last ten years alone Newcastle, and Liverpool & London have disappeared as separate entities and British Marine has demutualised.

In a global interconnected world shipowning is still an unusual business in which the owner has to endeavour to control an asset 'that sails thousands of miles away from his office'.[76] His ship operates in a complex environment and has to handle transactions with hundreds of professionals located in different parts of the globe and consequently 'competitiveness depends strongly on the ability to reduce the cost and the risk of these transactions as much as possible'. P&I may not be a large percentage of the operating costs of a ship but it is critical in enabling the movement of world trade. While the legal environment has become ever more restrictive in the wake of major disasters and yet more preventive measures are put in place, the claims will continue. Claims may have changed in size and scale over the last 100 years but the perils of the sea, human error and political events will continue to impact shipping and P&I insurance will continue to insure for the incidents no one foresaw.

Steamship takes much pride in its service to its members. This has been supported by comments from several owners interviewed for this book. Mr Souri had his first contact with Steamship in 1980 when he was in charge of the Iranian national fleet (IRISL) In his view the Club has made 'great endeavours to be client oriented and to demonstrate flexibility towards members' needs.'[77] While others have said that the Club understands the shipowner's perspective and is not hidebound by absolute rules. There have been plenty of examples of this over time and it is with good reason that Steamship has chosen 'A century of service to shipping' as its motto for its centenary year.

From Steamship's first Committee members to today's Board Directors, much may have changed in some ways but some aspects have remained the same. It is obvious that a good partnership between the Managers and the Club Members is essential, but what is also evident is that to be successful that relationship cannot afford to become complacent and both Directors and Managers have challenged one another from time to time. The Club has been fortunate in many of the personalities who have been leading lights in its history, but it is the unique combination of the whole, the staff of the Managers, at all levels, and the Members, particularly those who have served as Committee members or Directors, who have made it successful.

Board Meeting in Venice in 2005

The staff of Steamship Insurance Management Services Ltd, 2009

[76] Gelina Harlaftis and John Theotokas, 'European Family Firms in International Business: British and Greek Tramp-Shipping Firms', *Business History*, Vol. 46, No. 2. (April 2004), pp. 219-55

[77] Letter from M Souri 9th March 2009

Select Bibliography

Primary sources

Steamship Mutual Archive

Sailing Ship Mutual Insurance Association, minutes 9th July 1913 to 13th July 1964

Entrance fees & calls ledger 20th February 1907 and 20th February 1908

Thames Estuary & Coasting Sailing Barge, minutes 9th Jan 1912 to 1st April 1935

Coasting Vessel Mutual Marine Insurance Association, minutes 11th June 1935 to 29th June 1964

Attendance book 19th Sept 1933 to 14th November 1957

Steamship Mutual Underwriting Association Minutes 23rd April 1924 onwards

Steamship London Club Minutes 1970 onwards

Steamship London Circulars 1970 to 2008

Renewals Book (A S Stocken and J Plincke) 1951 to 1959

'Scrap book' (Rule books, circulars) 1906 to 1956

A Stocken & Co Annual Return 1954

Memorandum and Articles of Association:

   Sailing Ship 14th Feb 1906

   Steamship 16th Oct 1909

   Coasting 29th Feb 1912

   Thames Estuary 29th Feb 1912

   Alfred Stocken (Managers) 5th June 1940

   John Plincke (Brokers) 5th June 1940

David Hooper, Steamship History File 1909 to 1950

Howard Morgan, 'SSM History draft', July 1995

Anon, 'Steamship History notes', undated

S Crowe, 'SSM Club History notes', undated

L Spechel, Memoirs, 2008

Jim Howard-Smith, 'Notes on SSM History', c. 1983

Rule books for Britannia, British Marine, Liverpool & London, London Steamship, Neptune, Newcastle, North of England, Standard, Sunderland, UK, West of England, 1960–62

Private Collections

David Raddings: Gloucester & Severn Estuary Mutual Insurance Society Ltd Rule book, 1904

Raddings' correspondence regarding *Charlotte Kilner* and *Princess*

Sloman Neptun: Correspondence 1949 to 1950

Board of Trade wreck report for *Indian Enterprise*, 8th January 1951

Census Returns 1901 and 1911

British Parliamentary Papers (1907): Annual Statement of the Navigation and Shipping of the United Kingdom for 1906

British Parliamentary Papers (1810): Select Committee on Marine Insurance

Publications

Kelly's Post Office Directory 1909

Fairplay

Guernsey Evening Press

Lloyd's List

Lloyd's Register

Lloyd's Register Annual Report 1952

Lloyd's Register of Shipping Annual Report 1949/50

Lloyd's Register of Shipping Annual Report 1960

The Times

Western Mail 8th April 2009

Whitstable Times and Tankerton Press

Secondary Sources

Aldcroft, D.H., 'The Eclipse of British Coastal Shipping, 1913-21', *Journal of Transport History* VI, 1963, p. 24

Aldcroft, Derek Howard. 'The Depression in British Shipping, 1901-11', *Journal of Transport History*, 7:1 (1965), pp. 14-23

Andrews, Robert D'Arcy, *Braunton: Home of the Last Sailing Coasters*, (Braunton: Braunton & District Museum, 2007)

Armstrong, John. 'Some Aspects of the Business History of the British Coasting Trade'. *International Journal of Maritime History* (St John's, Newfoundland), 18:2 (2006), pp. 1-15

Armstrong, John. 'Climax and Climacteric: The British Coastal Trade, 1870–1930' in Starkey, David John; Jamieson, Alan G., *Exploiting the Sea: Aspects of Britain's Maritime Economy since 1870*, (Exeter: Exeter University Press, 1998), pp. 37-58

Bakka, Dag., *Gard: the Celebration of a Century, 1907–2007*, (Gard, 2007)

Bennet, Douglas, *Schooner Sunset: The Last British Sailing Coasters*, (Rochester: Chatham Publishing, 2001)

Boyce, Gordon H., *Co-operative Structures in Global Business*, (London: Routledge, 2001)

Brautaset, Camilla and Tenold, Stig, 'Globalisation and Norwegian Shipping Policy, 1850–2000', *Business History*, Sep 2008, Vol. 50 Issue 5, pp. 565-82

Broeze, Frank, *The Globalisation of the Oceans: Containerisation from the 1950s to the Present,* (St John's, Newfoundland: IMEHA, 2002)

Buckley, Jim, 'International Shipping and the Baltic Exchange' in Starkey, D. and Murphy, H., (eds), *Beyond Shipping and Shipbuilding,* (Hull: University of Hull, 2007), pp. 217-220

Corlett, E., *The Revolution in Merchant Shipping 1950–1980,* (HMSO/NMM, 1981)

Davies, P.N., 'British Shipping and World Trade: Rise and Decline 1820–1939' in *Business History of Shipping Strategy and Structure,* (Tokyo, 1985), pp. 39-85

Doe, Helen, *Jane Slade of Polruan,* (Truro: Truran, 2002)

Fryer, Martin, *A Newcastle Century: One Hundred Years of Newcastle P and I Association,* (Newcastle-upon-Tyne: Newcastle P & I Association, 1987)

Gardiner, R., ed., *The Golden Age of Shipping: The Classic Merchant Ship 1900–1960,* (Conway's History of the Ship, London, 1994)

Goss, R.O., *The Cost of Ships' Time,* (London, HMSO, 1974)

Greaves, Julian, 'Managing Decline: The Political Economy of British Shipping in the 1930s', *Journal of Transport History,* Vol. 28, No.1 (2007), pp. 57-74

Greenhill, B. *The Merchant Schooners,* (London:Conway Maritime Press, 1988)

Harlaftis, G., *A History of Greek Owned Shipping: The Making of an International Tramp Fleet, 1830 to Present Day,* (London; Routledge, 1996)

Harlaftis, G., *Greek Shipowners and Greece, 1945–1975,* (London; Athlone Press, 1993)

Harlaftis, Gelina and John Theotokas, 'European Family Firms in International Business: British and Greek Tramp-Shipping Firms', *Business History,* Vol. 46, No. 2 (April 2004), pp. 219-55

Hazlewood, Steven J., *P and I Clubs: Law and Practice,* (London: LLP, 2000)

Heaton, P.M., *Jack Billmeir: Merchant Shipowner,* (Newport, Starling Press, 1989)

Heaton, Paul, *Spanish Civil War Blockade Runners:* (Abergavenny; P M Heaton Publishing, 2006)

Imaizumi, Takatada, 'Transition of Shipowners' Liability Laws and Changes of P & I Clubs in the UK (Part 1)' *Yokohama Business Review,* Vol. X, No. 3 (1989), pp. 221-241

Imaizumi, Takatada, 'Transition of Shipowners' Liability Laws and Changes of P & I Clubs in the UK (Part 11-1)' *Yokohama Business Review,* Vol. XI, No. 2 (1990), pp. 108-25

Jamieson, A.G., 'An Inevitable Decline? Britain's Shipping and Shipbuilding Industries since 1930' in Starkey, David John; Jamieson, Alan G., *Exploiting the Sea: Aspects of Britain's Maritime Economy since 1870,* (Exeter: Exeter University Press, 1998), pp. 79-92

Jones, F.I.W., 'The German Challenge to British Shipping 1885–1914', *Mariner's Mirror,* 76 (1990), p. 151

Jones, Geoffrey, *Merchants to Multinationals: British Trading Companies in the Nineteenth and Twentieth Centuries* (Oxford: Oxford University Press, 2000)

Latham, Tim, *The Ashburner Schooners: The Story of the First Shipbuilders in Barrow-in-Furness* (Manchester: Ready Rhino Publications, 1991)

Ledwith, Frank, *Ships That Go Bump in the Night* (London: Robert Hale, 1974)

Levinson, M., *The Box: How the Shipping Container made the World Smaller and the World Economy Bigger'*, (Princeton: Princeton University Press, 2006)

Lindfelt, Lars (ed), *The Swedish Club over 125 years,* (Goteborg: The Swedish Club, 1997)

Lund, Jann T., *Skuld: 100 Years,* (Oslo: Assuranceforeningen Skuld, 1997)

Metaxas, B.N., *The Economics of Tramp Shipping,* (London: Athlone Press, 1971)

Miller, Michael B., 'Ship Agents in the Twentieth Century', in Boyce, G., Gorski, R. eds *Resources and Infrastructures in the Maritime Economy, 1500–2000,* (St Johns, Newfoundland, IMEHA 2002), pp. 5-22

Miller, Michael B., 'Maritime Networks in the Twentieth Century', *Business History Review,* Vol. 77, No. 1 (2003), pp. 1-32

Nurse, James. *The Nurse Family of Bridgwater & their Ships* (Carmania Press: London 1999)

Palmer, Sarah, 'The Indemnity in the London Marine Insurance Market, 1824-50' in Oliver M. Westall (ed) *The Historian and the Business of Insurance* (Manchester: Manchester University Press, 1984), pp. 74-94

Paterson, L., *Only Thirty Birthdays; British Marine Mutual, 1976–1996,* (London: BMM, 1996)

Perks, R.H., 'The Barge Builder: Horace Shrubsall of East Greenwich'. *Bygone Kent,* 20:2 (1999), pp. 86-94

Peterson, M.L.R., 'The Sea Venture', *Mariner's Mirror,* Vol 74 (Feb 1988), pp. 37-48

Pollard, S., 'Shipping and the British Economy since 1870: A Retrospective View' in Starkey, David John; Jamieson, Alan G., *Exploiting the Sea: Aspects of Britain's Maritime Economy since 1870,* (Exeter: Exeter University Press, 1998), pp. 93-103

Starkey, D.J., & Harlaftis, G., *Global Markets: The Internationalisation of the Sea Transport Industries since 1850* (St Johns, Newfoundland, 1998)

Stopford, Martin, *Maritime Economics,* (Abingdon: Routledge, 1997)

Sturmey, S.G., *British Shipping and World Competition,* (London, The Athlone Press, 1962)

Tenold, Stig, 'Exodus Explained- The Fate of Ships Sold from Norway, 1970–1987', *Mariner's Mirror,* Vol. 92, No. 3, (2006), pp. 300-08

Tenold, Stig, *Tankers in Trouble: Norwegian Shipping and the Crisis of the 1970s and 1980s,* (St Johns, Newfoundland: IMEHA 2006)

Thomson, Peter, 'Working a Thames Sailing Barge circa 1950', *Mariner's Mirror,* 81 (1995), pp. 457-62

Thompson, Peter, 'Bude: A Haven not without Risk', *Mariner's Mirror,* Vol. 87, (2001), pp. 316-24

Ward-Jackson, C.H., *Ships and Shipbuilders of a Westcountry Seaport: Fowey 1786–1939,* (Truro: Twelveheads Press, 1986)

Young, Peter, *Mutuality: The Story of the UK P&I Club,* (London: Thomas Miller & Co, 1995)

Author
Dr Helen Doe, FRSA

Helen is a Fellow of the Centre for Maritime Historical Studies at the University of Exeter. She gained her PhD in Maritime History from Exeter, where she previously gained her Masters in Maritime History. Her research interests are in the field of maritime business history. She has published several articles and her latest book, *Enterprising Women in Shipping in the Nineteenth Century*, will be published in September 2009.

She has for some years been a Trustee of the National Maritime Museum of Cornwall and is now the Chairman of the Editorial Board of *Troze*, their on-line journal. She is a Trustee of the *SS Great Britain*, a member of the British Commission for Maritime History, a Council member of the Navy Records Society, and was previously a Council member of the Society for Nautical Research (SNR). She is also a Fellow of the Royal Society of Arts.

Before studying at Exeter, she worked as a marketing consultant for a range of companies inside and outside the UK. Before that, her main career was in international sales and marketing with IBM.

www.helendoe.co.uk

Index